Straight and crooked thinking

ROBERT H. THOULESS
Reader Emeritus in the University of Cambridge

Pan Books London and Sydney

First published 1930 by Hodder and Stoughton Ltd
Revised and enlarged edition published 1953 by
Pan Books Ltd, Cavaye Place, London SW10 9PG
17th printing (revised and reset) 1974
22nd printing 1981
ISBN 0 330 24127 3
Copyright Robert H. Thouless 1930, 1953
© Robert H. Thouless 1974
Printed in Great Britain by
Richard Clay (The Chaucer Press) Ltd, Bungay, Suffolk

CONTENTS

PREFACE

IN ANY book on this subject, the author has to make the choice between taking his examples of crooked thinking from live controversial questions such as politics, and choosing them from the hackneyed and trivial sources favoured by the academic textbooks. There are many advantages in adopting the latter course. Most important of all is the fact that the illustration of a faulty argument by a reference to Socialism or disarmament tends to distract the reader's attention from the nature of the argument to the truth of the statement. For this reason it is impossible altogether to give up the use of trivial illustrations. Wherever it is possible, however, I have made my illustrations from living controversial issues and from arguments that are actually used in defence of them. This choice may give offence to some readers who find that I have held up to ridicule arguments in defence of positions that are dear to them. In such cases, however, they can replace them by illustrations of similar crooked thinking on the part of those with whom they disagree.

It is not necessary for a writer on crooked thinking to make the essentially dishonest claim that he is himself a model of straight thinking. We can only understand crooked thinking when we have followed it in our own minds as well as in the writings and speeches of others. So I have made little attempt to achieve an artificial impartiality on controversial questions, and I do not suppose that it will need any very great amount of insight for a reader to guess with a fair degree of probability what are my own convictions. Having guessed these, he can make allowances for my resulting prejudices and no harm will have been done. It must not be inferred, however, from the mere fact that I condemn an argument or a method of thought that I necessarily disagree with its conclusions. A sound conclusion may be supported by a bad argument.

When this book was brought out in a Pan edition in 1953, I made an extensive revision of it, expanding some parts and modifying others, also replacing some of its out-of-date illustrations by others of more contemporary interest. Controversial issues constantly change and some of the 1953 illustrative material has itself become somewhat out-of-date now. I have, therefore, made a considerable further revision, bringing in more illustrations from controversies of the present time. I have also thought it desirable to clarify some parts of the book that seemed to me to have been obscurely expressed and to cut out some sections that did not seem to me to be any longer of current interest.

R.H.T.

CHAPTER I

DIFFERENT WAYS OF USING LANGUAGE

WHEN I wrote the first version of the present book, I gave it the title *Straight and Crooked Thinking*; it might alternatively have been called *Straight and Crooked Communication*. Communication and thought are two closely related activities; they are two ways of using language. It has been said: 'Man is a talking animal; when he has no one to talk to, he talks to himself'. Talking to others is what we mean by 'communication'; talking to oneself is what we call 'thinking'. Talking to oneself is not the whole of thinking but it is that part of thinking in which language is used; it is the part we are here concerned with. Communication and thinking are obviously different activities but they are closely connected; crooked thinking leads to crooked communication and vice versa.

One of the ways in which confusion arises in thinking or communication is from confusion as to what we are doing in a particular act of communication or of thinking. There are a number of different ways in which we can use language:

(1) To give information about a fact, e.g. 'Kangaroos are found in Australia'.

(2) To ask for information as to fact, e.g. 'Are there kangaroos in New Guinea?'

(3) To indicate an emotional attitude, e.g. 'Spiders are revolting animals'.

(4) To indicate how a word is used, e.g. '"Marsupials" are animals with pouches'.

(5) To ask how a word is used, e.g. 'What is an "ungulate"?'

(6) To get someone to carry out an action e.g. 'Please pass the milk'.

These are, perhaps, the principal ways in which we use language, but there are also innumerable others, for example:

(7) To make poetry.
(8) To make a joke.
(9) To make a quarrel.
(10) To resolve a quarrel.
(11) To give a greeting.

Etc, etc.

These are what the philosopher Wittgenstein has called different 'language games'. One is perhaps more likely to be generally understood if one calls them different ways of using language. One source of crooked thinking or crooked communication is confusion between these different ways of using language. A somewhat sophisticated confusion to be discussed later (Chapter V) is that between the first and the fourth way of using language, between statements about facts and statements about the use of words.

There is a simpler and very common confusion between the first and the third ways of using language, between statements of fact and indications of emotional attitude. When someone says: 'Rover is a dog', he is doing no more than stating a fact; he is employing the first of the ways of using language described above.

Let us suppose that one of Rover's grandparents was a collie, another was an Irish terrier, another a fox terrier and the fourth a bulldog. These facts could be expressed by saying that he is a dog of mixed breed. Language would then still be used in the first manner of stating a fact. Suppose, however, that someone calls Rover a 'mongrel'. The matter is then more complicated. A word has been used which means the same, in fact, as does 'dog of mixed breed', but which also arouses in its hearers an attitude of disapproval towards the dog to whom it is applied. Thus the word 'mongrel' does not only indicate a fact, it also suggests an emotional attitude towards that fact; it combines the first and the third ways of using language in the above list. The use of the word goes beyond mere factual description since the attitude of disapproval that it suggests is something that belongs to the people discussing it and not to the dog that is being discussed. An animal which in the thought of its master is a noble animal of mixed breed may be a mongrel to his next-door neighbour.

In the same way, an individual of the dark-skinned races may be indicated factually as a 'black man', or with emotional disapproval and contempt as a 'nigger', a 'kaffir', or a 'coon'. Other words indicating an attitude of contempt towards members of other races are 'Yidd', 'Dago', 'Wop', etc. The use of such words cannot be tolerated in any reasonable discourse.

When we become aware of this difference between the *factual* and *emotional* uses of words, we shall notice that words which carry more or less strong suggestions of emotional attitudes are very common and are ordinarily used in the discussion of such controversial questions as those of politics, morals, and religion. This is one reason why men can go on discussing such questions without getting much nearer to a rational solution of them.

There is a well-known saying that the word 'firm' can be declined as follows: I am *firm*, thou art *obstinate*, he is *pig-headed*. This is a simple illustration of what is meant. 'Firm', 'obstinate', and 'pig-headed' all have the same factual meaning – that is, following one's own course of action and refusing to be influenced by other people's opinions. They have, however, different emotional meanings; 'firm' has an emotional meaning of strong approval, 'obstinate' of mild disapproval, 'pig-headed' of strong disapproval. If we wanted to find an emotionally neutral term that would convey the same idea without expressing either approval or disapproval, we should say perhaps 'X is *not easily influenced*'.

We can put this in another way. 'I am firm' is equivalent to saying 'I am not easily influenced and that is a good thing'; 'Thou art obstinate' is the same thing as 'Thou art not easily influenced and that is rather a bad thing'; 'He is pig-headed' means 'He is not easily influenced and that is a very bad thing'. We do not in ordinary conversation say explicitly whether we think the things we are talking about are good or bad; we can convey that by facial expression, by gesture, or by the tone of our voice. In writing, we have none of these means of expressing our emotional attitudes, but we still manage to avoid the necessity for saying 'This is a good thing' and 'That is a bad thing' by choosing words that imply opinions of goodness and badness, such as 'firm', 'obstinate', etc.

Such words are, no doubt, useful but they are a danger to reasonable thinking. In times when we are at war, our thought is dominated by emotional attitudes of approval of our own forces and war aims and of disapproval of those of our enemies. Then we are much inclined to the use of emotional language. We may talk of the *spirit* of our own soldiers and the *mentality* of the enemy soldiers, of the *heroism* of our own troops and the *foolhardiness* of the enemy. When peace comes and we look back on the facts more objectively, we can realize that a *spirit* and a *mentality* are factually the same, but the one word has an emotional meaning of approval while the other expresses disapproval. We can realize too that a soldier going forward under shell-fire to probable death is doing the same thing whether he is one of our own soldiers or one of the enemy's, and that to distinguish between them by applying the word *foolhardiness* to the action of the one and *heroism* to that of the other is to misrepresent reality by using words to make an emotional distinction between two actions which are factually identical.

Such thinking in wartime may do much harm by leading humane people to condone cruelty. When the ordinarily liberal-minded Swinburne wrote a poem during the Boer War on the death of a British officer who had been blamed for the bad condition of the camps in which the Boer women and children were interned, he said:

> Nor heed we more than he what liars dare say
> Of mercy's holiest duties left undone
> Towards *whelps* and *dams* of *murderous* foes whom none
> Save we had spared or feared to starve and slay.

Whelps and *dams* clearly mean in fact *children* and *wives*, with the added meaning of the emotional attitude adopted towards the females and young of wild beasts, while *murderous* means no more in fact than that our foes killed us when they could (as we also killed them), with the added emotional meaning of an attitude towards them which is our attitude to those who are guilty of murder.

Swinburne was not, of course, himself in charge of a prison camp of Boer women and children. No doubt if he had been, he would have administered it in a humane fashion and would not have thought of its inmates as 'whelps' and 'dams'. The users of language may feel less responsibility for how they use language than do those who make decisions as to what is to be done. Yet the danger of the use of such language in communication is that it may become part of the thought of those whose decisions affect the lives or well-being of the people it describes. An American officer accused of shooting women and children in the Vietnam war justified his action by saying: 'they were enemy, not people'.

Lorenz has pointed out how much less lasting is the

aggressiveness of wolves than is that of men. Wolves fight with ferocity, but when one is clearly getting the better of the fight the beaten wolf carries out an appeasement ceremony and the fight stops. It does not continue to the death nor does the victorious wolf go on to attack the female and cubs of the defeated wolf. Perhaps the point is that the wolf just fights, he does not talk about it to other wolves or to himself. He has no emotionally charged language to keep his aggressive impulses active when the immediate occasion for them has passed.

The use of language in stimulating aggressive impulses can be illustrated by a report published early in June 1971 of an incident in Vietnam in which twenty-four women and children were reported to have been shot by American soldiers. A technician trying to report the incident to his superiors was told: 'A gook is a gook. If it's got slanty eyes, kill the bastard.' Language of this kind can be used by a man, not by a wolf. It distorts thought about the enemy and may lead to terrible distortions of behaviour. We cannot hope to avoid atrocities when soldiers are led to think like that; perhaps something can be done to persuade both soldiers and civilians not to think in that way.

Accounts of wars and revolutions are rich sources for the study of the misuse of words with emotional meanings, so we are not surprised to read in a book on the French Commune that large numbers of the regular troops were *assassinated* during the street fighting by the communards, while a much larger number of the latter were *summarily executed* by the regulars. In order to reduce this to a statement of objective fact, it is necessary that the one word 'killed' should be used in place both of *assassinated* and *summarily executed*.

Similarly, during the fighting between the Red and the White forces in Russia after the Bolshevik revolution, most of our newspapers sympathized with the anti-Bolsheviks and told us of the *atrocities* of the Bolsheviks and of the *wise severity* of the White commanders. Examination of the details (often possible only long afterwards) shows that the objective facts of an *atrocity* and of *wise severity* are much the same, and that they are not the kind of objective facts which will call out an emotion of approval in a humane person.

A similar choice of words will be noticed in political discussion. A fluent and forcible speech delivered by one of our own party is *eloquent*, a similar speech by one of the opposite party is *bombastic* – again two words with the same objective meaning but with the opposite emotional meanings of approval and strong disapproval. The practical proposals of the opposition, moreover, are *panaceas* – a highly emotional word calling out the strongly disapproving emotions which we feel for those quack patent medicines which make extravagant claims. Those who show enthusiasm in support of proposals with which a speaker disagrees are *extremists*, while those showing similar enthusiasm on his own side are called *staunch*. If a politician wishes to attack some new proposal he has a battery of these and other words with emotional meanings at his disposal. He speaks of 'this suggested *panacea* supported only by the *bombast* of *extremists*', and the proposal is at once discredited in the minds of the majority of people, who like to think of themselves as moderate, distrustful of panaceas, and uninfluenced by windy eloquence. Also we may notice that it has been discredited without the expenditure of any real thought, for of real objective argument there is none, only the manipulation of words calling out emotion.

It is not, however, only in warfare and politics that such words are used in order to influence opinion more easily than can be done by words embodying real thought. Thinking on religious questions is also often made difficult by the persistence with which religious controversialists use emotionally toned words. Thus a man who holds firmly a definite system of religious beliefs may be called a *bigot* by those who disapprove of him and a *man of faith* by those who approve of him. *Strong in the faith of our fathers* and *shackled by an outworn creed* are phrases which may have identical factual meanings but opposite emotional meanings. The emotional meaning of each of them confuses thought by directing attention away from the point that, in order to decide whether we ought to hold a body of beliefs, we have to consider only whether they are true; the fact that they were believed by people in the past is not in itself a sufficient reason for holding them and is a still worse reason for rejecting them.

In criticism of pictures and books we may also find interference with exact thinking by the use of emotional language. Some years ago, when such subjects were less freely discussed than they are now, a woman novelist wrote a book *The Well of Loneliness* about female homosexuality. This was savagely attacked in a newspaper article in the following words: 'Its *vicious plea* for the acknowledgement and *condonation of sexual perversity*, and the grounds on which it is based, loosen the very *sheet-anchor of conduct*.' This passage calls out such strong emotions of abhorrence that most readers will be content to condemn the novel without further inquiry. Yet the effect is gained entirely by the choice of words with emotional meanings. It happens to deal with a subject on which emotions are strong, so a dispassionate examination is all the more necessary. We note that the word *plea* means simply an argument, plus a suggestion of repugnance for the kind of argument used, that *condonation* is tolerance plus an emotional suggestion that such toleration is indefensible; that *sexual* means something in the life of love of which we disapprove, and that a *perversity* is an unusualness plus an emotional suggestion of abhorrence. The loosening of a *sheet-anchor* is a metaphor implying change and suggesting to a landsman the emotion of fear, while *conduct* is simply behaviour of which we approve.

So reduced to its bare bones of statement of objective fact

(ignoring for a moment the special difficulties raised by the word *vicious*) the passage becomes: 'Its argument for the acknowledgement and tolerance of unusualness in the life of love, and the grounds on which it is based, change the principles of behaviour.' This clearly is an important statement if is true, but is not enough in itself to condemn the book, because undoubtedly our principles of behaviour do need changing from time to time. We can only decide intelligently whether or not they need changing in the particular case under discussion when we have made a dispassionate examination of what the proposed changes are and why they are defended. As in all other cases, discussion of the question with emotionally charged words obscures the problem and makes a sensible decision difficult or impossible.

The word *vicious* has some special difficulties of its own. Certainly this word has an emotional meaning of strong disapproval, but in this case we cannot perform the operation of replacing it by an emotionally neutral word which has otherwise the same meaning since no such word can be found. If we want to express the same meaning, we can call the book 'bad', 'corrupt', or 'evil', but whatever word we choose will have the same emotional meaning of disapproval. Can we then say that such words have no place in exact thinking since they do not state facts but are only used to arouse emotion?

This is a problem about which there has been much dispute. Some philosophers have maintained that all such words as 'vicious', 'bad', 'good', 'beautiful', and 'ugly' only indicate the speaker's own emotional reactions towards certain actions and things, and not properties of those actions and things themselves. But when we see a man carry out a mean or selfish action and say that his action is 'bad', we certainly intend to say something about the action itself and not merely about how we feel about it. This is clear from the fact that it makes sense to say, 'I think swearing is bad although I don't disapprove of it myself', just as it makes sense to say, 'That picture is, no doubt, beautiful although I don't happen to like it myself.' So there does not seem to be sufficient ground for asserting that we do not succeed in saying something meaningful about a book itself when we call it 'vicious' but have only said something about our own feelings.

If, however, we agree that the statement that a book is vicious has a meaning which is not merely an emotional meaning, we must also agree that it is not quite the same kind of meaning as a simple statement of outside fact such as 'This is a book'. Whether the book is good or bad is a real question, but it is a question peculiarly difficult to decide. Our own statement one way or the other is likely to be nothing but a reflection of our own personal prejudices and to have, therefore, no sort of scientific exactness. At the same time, such words certainly arouse strong emotions and should, therefore, be used sparingly in honest argument. The use of words implying moral judgements in the course of argument is very generally an attempt to distort the hearers' view of the truth by arousing emotions.

If we are trying to decide a simple question of fact, such words should be left out, because it is easier to settle one question at a time. If a man is accused of poisoning his wife, the prosecuting attorney should not say, 'This *scoundrel* who hounded his wife to her grave.' The question to be decided is whether the man did poison his wife. If he did, he is a 'scoundrel' undoubtedly, but calling him a scoundrel does not help to decide the question of fact. On the contrary, it makes a correct decision more difficult by rousing emotions of hatred for the accused in the minds of the jury. Another obvious objection to the use of the word 'scoundrel' before the man is convicted, which puts it in the ranks of 'crooked thinking', is that it 'begs the question' or assumes what is to be proved. The man is only a scoundrel if he is guilty, and yet the word has been used in the course of an argument to prove that he is guilty.

These two objections can be urged against the word 'vicious' in the condemnation of a book quoted above. It calls up strong emotions making a just decision of the nature of the book difficult, and it assumes exactly what the article professes to prove, that the book was a bad one.

The use of emotionally toned words is not, of course, always to be condemned. It is always harmful when the situation is one which requires that factual information should be communicated or that people should be enabled to think clearly so that they may decide on a disputed factual matter. In poetry, on the other hand (as has been pointed out by Charlton in *The Art of Literary Study*) emotional language has a proper place because in poetry (as in some kinds of prose) the arousing of various emotions may be an important part of the purpose for which the words are used.

In *The Eve of St Agnes* Keats has written:

> Full on this casement shone the wintry moon,
> And threw warm gules on Madeline's fair breast.

These are beautiful lines. Let us notice how much of their beauty follows from the proper choice of emotionally coloured words and how completely it is lost if these words are replaced by neutral ones. The words with strikingly emotional meanings are *casement*, *gules*, *Madeline*, *fair*, and *breast*. *Casement* means simply a kind of window with emotional associations. *Gules* is the heraldic name for red, with the suggestion of romance which accompanies all heraldry. *Madeline* is simply a girl's name, but one calling out favourable emotions absent from a relatively commonplace name. *Fair* simply means, in fact, that her skin was white or uncoloured – a necessary condition for the colours of the window to show – but also *fair* implies warm emotional preference for an uncoloured skin rather than one which is yellow, purple, black, or any of the other colours which skin might be. *Breast* has similar emotional meanings, and the aim of scientific description might have been equally well attained if it had been replaced by such a neutral word as *chest*.

Let us now try the experiment of keeping these two lines in a metrical form, but replacing all the emotionally coloured words by others that are as emotionally neutral as possible while conveying the same factual meaning. We may, for example, write:

> Full on this window shone the wintry moon,
> Making red marks on Jane's uncoloured chest.

No one will doubt that all of its poetic value has been knocked out of the passage by these changes. Yet the lines still have the same factual meaning; it is only the emotional meaning that has been destroyed.

Now if Keats had been writing a scientific description for a textbook on physics instead of a poem, it would have been necessary for him to have used some such coldly objective terms as those into which we have just translated his lines. Such emotionally charged phrases as *warm gules* and *fair breast* would only have obscured the facts to which the scientist exactly but unbeautifully refers when he speaks of 'the selective transmission of homogeneous light by pigmented glass.'

Nor is it reasonable to condemn all use of emotionally charged words in ordinary conversation. Conversation would be dull if it did not include indications of how the speaker felt about the things he was talking about. These indications are provided in various ways, partly by the use of emotionally charged words, partly by changes in intonation. No one would wish to eliminate this factor in conversation although one may have doubts about its usefulness in public discussion.

Even emotional oratory has, no doubt, its place. I would suggest, however, that this place is not where it is often found, as a technique of persuasion when a responsible decision is to be made. It may, on the other hand, be an invaluable stimulus to action when what is required is to persuade people to do something which it is already agreed is right or at least necessary. So one may justify the emotional oratory of Winston Churchill during the Second World War. Then the situation required the behaviour of enduring hardship and the taking of action necessary to survival. The same sort of oratory is less useful in times of peace when what is required is that people shall make responsible decisions as to what is to be done. Emotional communication and thinking about such practical problems as taxation, public or private ownership, tensions between different nations or forms of religion, immigration, and abortion, are as much out of place as would be a chemical formula in a poem. Effective democracy requires that people shall make decisions by a process of calm appraisal of the facts. Such calm appraisal is obstructed by the use of emotional oratory in presentation of the facts. After the decision, action follows, and into that action may be put all the emotion which, in an ideal democracy, has been excluded from the preliminary process of decision-making.

The psychological purpose of emotion (anger, fear, benevolence, etc) is to make people act effectively. It muddles thought but it stimulates action. The ideal is to think calmly and to act effectively. Let us think calmly and factually about such things as poverty, oppression of minorities, loss of liberty, war, unrestricted population growth, and environmental contamination. If we decide calmly and rationally that these are great evils which may be overcome by our efforts, then we may usefully put into action directed towards the overcoming of them all the passion of which we are capable.

The development of the exact thinking of modern science

has been very largely a process of getting rid of all terms conveying emotional attitudes and using only those which unemotionally indicate objective facts. It was not always so. The old alchemists called gold and silver 'noble' metals, and thought that this emotionally coloured word indicated something belonging to the metals themselves from which their properties could be deduced. Other metals were called 'base'. Although these terms have survived as convenient labels for the modern chemist they carry none of their old emotional significance.

In popular discussion, on the other hand, such words are still used with their full emotional meaning, as when the 'nobility' of man is contrasted with his alleged 'base' origin. In this respect, popular biological discussion differs from that of the textbook and the laboratory, in which are used terms almost as devoid of emotional meaning as those of physics or chemistry.

When we turn to political and international thinking, we are further from straight scientific thinking. Such words as: 'progress', 'liberty', 'democracy', 'fascist', 'reactionary', 'racist', 'liberal', and many others are used in political thinking and communication in such a way that they carry more of emotional than of factual meaning. So long as words so used are the ordinary terms of rival politicians, how can we hope to think straight in national and international affairs? If a chemist doing an experiment depended on such thought processes as a nation uses in selecting its rulers or in deciding on peace or war with other nations, he would blow up his laboratory. This however, would be a trivial disaster in comparison with what may result from emotional thinking in politics. Better have a hundred chemical laboratories blown up than the whole of civilization!

We must look forward to the day when the thinking about political and international affairs will be as unemotional and as scientific as that about the properties of numbers or the atomic weights of elements. The spirit of impartial investigation of facts unswayed by irrelevant emotions has given us great advances in the sciences. Its triumphs will be even greater when it is applied to the most important affairs of life. We shall be able to discuss and settle such questions as public v private ownership, control of atomic weapons, and disarmament treaties as succesfully as physicists have discussed and settled Einstein's theory of relativity.

Emotional oratory, as has already been pointed out, has its legitimate place. If there is no doubt about what we ought to do, then emotional oratory may be properly used to stir us to do it. Such oratory is out of place when the problem before us is to make a decision, as in a political election. The theory of democracy is that in an election the people have to make a rational decision. If they had to be stirred to do something arduous and distasteful (as in a war or a revolution), then emotional oratory would be a useful means of getting them to do it. Since what they are required to do in an election is to think clearly and come to a sensible decision, the use of emotional language in political speakers is altogether to be condemned, since it makes clear thinking and sensible decision more difficult.

However, political speakers are more interested in creating conviction than in promoting clear thinking, so they will go on using emotional language. Nothing that the psychologist can say will stop them. On the other hand, we can educate ourselves in such a way as to make us relatively immune to the influence of such language if we become aware of what is being done and, instead of responding with the emotions that the speaker intends, think of the factual meaning of what he is saying and discount its emotional meaning.

So that we may become able to do this, I suggest that we should try to do some practical work on the subject of this chapter instead of being content merely to read it. If you were studying botany, you would not merely read books on botany, you would gather plants from the hedges and weeds from your garden, dissecting them, examining them with a micro-scope or magnifying glass, and drawing them in your note-book. Psychology too should be studied by practical methods. Emotional thinking is to be found in the leading articles of newspapers, in the words of people carrying on discussions on political, religious, or moral questions, and in the speeches made by public men when these deal with controversial mat-ters. In order to understand it, we should collect specimens for study and dissection.

The practical exercise which I recommend is one that I have already performed on some passages in which truth seemed to be obscured by emotional thinking. I suggest that readers should copy out controversial passages from newspapers, books, or speeches which contain emotionally coloured words. Then they should underline all the emotional words, after-wards rewriting the passages with the emotional words re-placed by neutral ones. Examine the passage then in its new form in which it merely states facts without indicating the writer's emotional attitude towards them, and see whether it is still good evidence for the proposition it is trying to prove. If it is, the passage is a piece of straight thinking in which emotionally coloured words have been introduced merely as an ornament. If not, it is crooked thinking, because the con-clusion depends not on the factual meaning of the passage but on the emotions roused by the words.

When we condemn such a use of emotional words in writ-ings and speeches, we must remember that this is a symptom of a more deep-seated evil – their prevalenece in our own private, unexpressed thinking. Many of our highly coloured political speakers whose speeches stir us as we are stirred by romantic poetry show themselves unable to think calmly and objectively on any subject. They have so accustomed themselves to think in emotionally toned words that they can no longer think in any other way. They should have been poets or professional orators, but certainly not statesmen.

We can best guard ourselves against being misled by emotional oratory by making sure that our own minds do not get into such a state. It is not that we should never use emotional words in our thinking but that we should know when we are doing so and have a method of counteracting their effects. When we catch ourselves thinking in emotional phraseology, let us form a habit of translating our thoughts into emotionally neutral words. So we can save ourselves from ever being so enslaved by emotional words and phrases that they prevent us from thinking objectively when we need to do so – that is, whenever we have to come to a decision on any debatable matter.

In the same way, I suggest that those who wish to learn more of the nature of crooked thinking should, after the reading of each of the later chapters, try to collect specimens of the tricks described from the source I have mentioned. In some cases I shall suggest practical operations which can be carried out on them in order to make clear the nature of the crooked thinking (as, for example, in Chapter X the provision of a new setting for doubtful propositions which run along the lines of our own thought habits). These operations should be carried out on the material you have collected. In this way it will be possible to gain a better mastery of the subject and a better protection against your own intellectual exploitation by unscrupulous speakers than by merely reading books.

The intention of this book is primarily practical. Its main purpose is not to stimulate intellectual curiosity but to increase awareness of the processes of crooked thinking and crooked communication and to provide safeguards against these. It would not have succeeded in its object if it merely led its readers to study books about logic. The test of its success is rather whether it makes it less easy for one of its readers to be persuaded by a salesman to buy a vacuum cleaner or an encyclopaedia that he (or she) does not want, and less easy for a political speaker to influence his way of voting by such irrational means as the use of emotional language or confident affirmation. More importantly I hope it will make it less easy for the reader to hate the enemy, whoever he may be at the moment, communist, boche, or gook, with that blind lack of understanding that comes from the various forms of crooked thinking about him.

CHAPTER II

ALL AND SOME

MANY YEARS ago, when I was living in Scotland, I passed through an area in which there was to be voting on whether to continue local prohibition of the sale of alcoholic drinks. There I saw the following poster: IF LIBERTY IS LOST, SLAVERY REIGNS: VOTE REPEAL. The first part of this poster is an argument. As often happens in practice, a great part of the argument is left out, but we can easily supply the missing part, and the result is an argument which, at first sight, looks a correct one. It would run like this: (1) A condition in which liberty is lost is one in which slavery reigns, (2) Prohibition is a condition in which liberty is lost, (3) Therefore, prohibition is a condition in which slavery reigns.

Now, this has the general form of a correct argument, and the statements (1) and (2) are both correct, so the conclusion must also be correct, provided that identical terms in (1) and (2) have identical meanings. This important provision is not fulfilled, however, so the conclusion is not proved. Moreover, whatever may be our views on the drink question, we see that the conclusion is wrong in fact. Inability to buy a glass of beer may be a bad thing but it is not slavery.

The fallacy lies in the omission of the word 'all' or 'some' in front of 'liberty'. Statement (1) is only true if 'all' is the missing word, while (2) is only true if 'some' is the missing word. The fallacy is quite clear in the extended form of the argument, but it is concealed in its original shortened form,

'If liberty is lost, slavery reigns'. It is true that under prohibition some liberty is lost – the liberty to buy alcoholic drink. But the argument suggests, quite untruly, that under prohibition all liberty is lost, for it is only when all liberty is lost that slavery can be said to reign.

This can be put in a more general way by saying that a common form of dishonest argument is the statement 'A is B' when 'Some A is B' would be true but 'All A is B' is what the hearer is meant to accept as what has been asserted. The world of propaganda and of argumentation is full of such statements. Our fathers refused to allow women to vote at parliamentary elections because 'women are politically incapable'. Undoubtedly some women are incapable of making sensible political decisions (as are some men), but certainly not all. As we have seen, Swinburne condoned the bad conditions of the camps in which Boer women and children were interned during the South African War because our foes were 'murderous'. Yet he could not reasonably have maintained more than that 'some' were murderous, while his plea was only reasonable if 'all' were murderous. Massacres of Jews in the Middle Ages, of aristocrats in the French Revolution, the persecution of minority groups in various countries in our own times – these are all examples of the readiness of men to act on the proposition that 'All Xs are evil' when X stands for men of another nation, race, or creed. Yet it is apparent to the impartial observer that the truth is merely that 'Some Xs are evil' (as equally are some not-Xs). Cruelty and injustice are resulting now, as they have throughout the history of the world, from this piece of crooked thinking.

It is not, of course, the case that all general statements of the form 'All Xs are Y' must necessarily be untrue. That would be absurd. I am only concerned to point out that they very often are untrue and that we may be led to overlook their untruth if the word 'all' is left out. Then they escape challenge because it looks as if they meant 'Some Xs are Y' although they are used in argument as if 'All Xs are Y' were true.

One reason why we are so much inclined to say or to imply 'all' in a sentence which would be true with the word 'some' is that a sentence with 'some' says so little. Suppose that we say quite truthfully: 'Some red-haired people are bad-tempered'. We have said so little that it was hardly worth saying at all, for so also are some people bad-tempered who are not red-haired, and some people are certainly not bad-tempered who are red-haired. So we have not said much when we have merely said, 'Some red-haired people are bad-tempered'; not enough for it to be worth while for a red-haired person to argue against the proposition.

Clearly we need some way of saying something about the connection between bad temper and redness of hair which means more than the simple statement with 'some' and yet is not the same as the obviously untrue statement with 'all'. This statement, when we have it, may, of course, be true or false. The first step is to consider exactly what we want to say; then we can find out whether or not it is true.

There is, in fact, such a form of statement. It is found even in everyday speech, as when a man may say: 'I think that red-haired people are more inclined to be bad-tempered than other people'. Or, of course, he may think that they are less inclined to be bad-tempered than other people. A man who has taught himself to think in such terms is less likely to fall into the type of error we have been discussing. Also he is more likely to appreciate that it is difficult to get evidence good enough to prove such a statement, and that one cannot get very good evidence from the casual observations of everyday life.

Such social sciences as psychology, economics, and sociology are much concerned with relationships of this kind. Human beings differ from each other too much for it to be likely that in the sciences dealing with them one will find many true statements in the form 'All Xs are Y'. Much more commonly the form of statement that has to be used in these sciences is of the kind: 'There is a tendency for Xs to be Y'. If we say that there is a tendency for red-haired people to be bad-tempered, we do not mean that all red-haired people are bad-tempered, and we do not imply that all people not red-haired are good-tempered. We do not even mean to imply that there are more red-haired bad-tempered people than there are bad-tempered people who are not red-haired. What is meant is that there is a larger proportion of bad-tempered people amongst the red-haired than amongst the people whose hair is not red. In other words, any person who has red hair is more likely to be a bad-tempered person than one who has not red hair.

We have now got a reasonable form of statement to inquire about. It still may not be true. If we wanted to discover whether it is true or not we should have to make some such investigation as the following. Let us suppose that we studied a random sample of a thousand people – a large enough group to be taken as a fair sample of the population as a whole. Let us suppose that we divided these into a group of 200 who had red hair and 800 who had not. Then let us suppose that we divided each of these groups into those who were and those who were not bad-tempered, and found 50 bad-tempered people amongst the red-haired and 100 amongst the not red-haired. We have now divided our thousand people into four classes, and every one of the thousand must fall into one or other of these classes. The result is summarized in the diagram on the following page.

Now these figures contain a complete answer to our question: Do red-haired people tend to be bad-tempered? Let us examine them carefully and see what they mean. There are twice as many bad-tempered people amongst the not red-haired as amongst the red-haired. But this does not mean that red-haired people are less likely to be bad-tempered than others because there is a smaller total number of the red-haired. In fact, one-quarter of the red-haired are bad-tempered and only one-eighth of the others. So the answer to our question indicated by these figures is 'Yes'. It appears that a book-maker could safely give you odds of about seven to one against a particular person without red hair being bad-tempered, but he could only offer you about three to one against a particular red-haired person being bad-tempered. The chance of a red-haired person being bad-tempered will be just double the chance of a not red-haired person being bad-tempered.

50	150
BAD-TEMPERED	not bad-tempered
RED-HAIRED	RED-HAIRED
100	700
BAD-TEMPERED	not bad-tempered
not red-haired	not red-haired

The figures given above are not, of course, genuine ones. They were invented by me as an illustration of what was meant by a tendency for Xs to be Y. So far as I know, the necessary statistical research into the association between red hair and bad temper has never been done; if it were done, I do not suppose it would show any tendency whatever for red-haired people to be more likely to be bad-tempered than the not red-haired.

The method of argument given above is one that will be

familiar to those who have studied statistical methods. I have given only the elementary part of the argument and omitted complications which would have to be considered by the research worker who was investigating such a problem as this. In particular, he would have to consider whether the proportions in his four classes indicated a real relationship between the two characteristics he was investigating or whether they might be 'chance' effects, that is, an accidental property of the sample he studied. Instructions on how to discover this are to be found in any textbook of statistical methods. In fact with a sample as large as 1,000 and a disproportion as great as 50:150 and 100:700, he would be entirely justified in drawing the conclusion that there was a real tendency for the two characteristics of red hair and bad temper to go together.

If we realize that this is the kind of evidence that would be required to justify the conclusion that red-haired people tend to be bad-tempered, we see how absurd it would be if two men set themselves to argue on the question of whether red-haired people were bad-tempered, and one of them said they were and 'proved' it merely by pointing to members of the red-haired, bad-tempered class and of the non-red-haired, non-bad-tempered class, while his opponent similarly 'proved' his case that red-haired people were not bad-tempered by pointing to the members of the non-bad-tempered, red-haired class and the bad-tempered, non-red-haired class. It would be about as easy for the second man as for the first, because in our group of 1000 he would have 100 of the one class and 150 of the other to point to. Yet it is as clear as it can be that neither of these two men would be proving his case at all, and also that the case could not be proved by the kind of argument they are using – a kind of argument we may call 'proof by selected instances.'

This is a trivial example but the principles involved apply also to questions of more moment. Suppose, for example, that the figures were those of the numbers of cigarette-smokers and non-cigarette-smokers who died of lung cancer. If in a properly selected sample, it were found that of 200 cigarette-smokers 50 died of lung cancer within a specified period whereas amongst 800 non-smokers of cigarettes 100 died of lung cancer within the same period of time, this would be sufficient proof that smokers of cigarettes were more likely to die of lung cancer. This distribution of figures would not itself be enough to prove that cigarette smoking caused lung cancer since there are two other ways in which it could be explained. It might be the result of the fact of suffering from lung cancer causing the sufferers to smoke cigarettes. It might also be the result of the fact that certain people differed from others in some respect that made them more likely to smoke cigarettes and also more likely to die of lung cancer. The first of these alternative explanations has, in this case, generally been regarded as too improbable for serious consideration, and the second is the one that has been put forward by those who do not accept the explanation that cigarette smoking is a cause of lung cancer. The figures actually obtained on this problem (which, of course, are not those shown on p 31) do, in fact, make it clear that there is a real association between cigarette smoking and the development of lung cancer. These figures do not in themselves prove that cigarette smoking causes lung cancer although they suggest this as a possible explanation; there are other researches which point strongly to the conclusion that it is also the right explanation.

There are many other disputed questions to which the same considerations apply. When, for example, we are at war with another nation or when we are in that state of tension now referred to as a 'cold war', we are inclined to think of the enemy people as bad. Indeed their supposed badness is one of the reasons for fighting a war to the end and for making harsh peace terms when it is over, as it is also for refusing to make the friendly gesture which might ease the tension of a cold war.

Yet we cannot suppose that all the people of the enemy nation are bad since we have known some of them personally and found them good and kindly people. We may, however, remain convinced that there is a strong tendency for the enemy people to be bad. Clearly the sociological measurements necessary to establish this tendency have not been made, and there is no sufficient rational ground for asserting it rather than the contrary proposition that as large a proportion of good and kindly people are to be found amongst the enemy nationals as anywhere else.

This is clearly a question on which none of us can bring forward the numerical evidence which would alone constitute sound proof. There are other questions on which the required numerical evidence is available, but which are nevertheless argued by the crude and inaccurate method of selected instances. We may take as an example the problem of whether capital punishment is an effective preventative of murder. Upholders of capital punishment can point to countries which have no capital punishment and a large number of murders, and those which have capital punishment and a small number of murders. Their opponents can point to countries with no capital punishment and few murders and to others with capital punishment and many murders. This is merely proof by selected instances and carries us no further. The real proof is an examination of the numerical relationships of all of these four classes such as we made earlier for the problem of bad temper and red hair, and this examination does not appear to indicate any association between the frequency of murder in a country and the capital punishment of murderers in that country.

There is a wide range of controversial statements often discussed in newspapers on which discussion can be interminable because the form of the statement is one in which there is no indication of whether 'all' or 'some' is meant. Examples of such statements are: 'The city child is more intelligent than the country child' (or, alternatively, 'The country child is sharper than the town child'), 'The black man is less intelligent than the white man', 'Women are less logical than men', 'The American is an individualist', 'The Australian is physically fit'. All of these statements are meaningless as they stand, and cannot sensibly be either asserted or denied. They are meaningless because the subject is indeterminate. There is not one city child but many. Some of these are highly intelligent, more of them are of about ordinary intelligence, some are imbecile. This is also true of country children. In the same way, some black men are intellectually brilliant while some white men are not. Some women are illogical but so are some men; some women are professors of logic at universities. Some Australians are physically fit, some walk with crutches, some are in hospitals for the disabled.

No doubt all these statements are made by people who really mean something else, and although they are nonsense in the form in which they are stated, they could be replaced by other statements which make sense and which a quantitative investigation might prove to be true or false. What then is at the back of the minds of those who say: 'The black man is less intelligent than the white man'. If we replace it by the statement: 'Every black man is less intelligent than every white man', we have said something which makes sense but which is manifestly false.

If we want a form of statement which is meaningful and which might be true or false, we must use some such form of words as that already discussed: 'There is a tendency for black men to be less intelligent than white men', This statement is meaningful but it may not be true; whether it is true or not can only be settled by the results of measurements by suitable intelligence tests of a large random sample of black people compared with similar measurements for a comparable sample of white people. The result of such a comparison might be to show that either one of the two groups had a higher average score than the other. Alternatively it might show that there was no measurable difference between the two groups. In the first case, one would also examine the figures to see how big the difference is, bearing in mind that a small average difference does not mean that there will not be people of high intelligence in both groups.

This is not a question to which one would expect a very clear-cut answer if one considers the wide range of difference in the black-skinned people between the highly civilized Ethiopians and the primitive Australian aborigines, and the wide range amongst the white-skinned people between the civilized Europeans and the primitive Ainus of Japan. A considerable amount of research has been done on this topic but its results are of somewhat doubtful interpretation since such differences as have been found may be the result of cultural differences rather than of racial differences. It is, at any rate, clear that if there is any tendency for intelligence to vary with skin colour it is a small one; if we want to know how intelligent a man is, we cannot do so reliably by looking at the colour of his skin.

There are other problems of the same kind the answer to which is not known because no one has yet overcome the difficulties of getting the information necessary for their solution. 'How far does our present use of imprisonment as a punishment succeed in decreasing crime?', 'Are State-managed commercial enterprises more or less efficient than privately managed enterprises?', and so forth. These seem to be questions which could be answered by sociological research, but this research has not yet been carried out. It does not follow, however, that on such questions we must have no opinions. On practical questions of urgent importance we must make up our minds one way or the other even when we know that the evidence is incomplete. To refuse to make up our minds is equivalent to deciding to leave things as they are (which is just as likely as any other to be the wrong solution).

But the fact that we must make up our minds in practice is no reason for failing to think straight on such questions by mistaking incomplete for complete evidence. We must not suppose that our case can be proved by merely selecting instances favourable to our view while we ignore other instances. If, for example, we are arguing in favour of private enterprise, it is not enough merely to give selected instances of unsuccessful State enterprises and of successful private ones. Nor must we think that our case is disproved if our opponents similarly select instances of successful State enterprises and private businesses that have failed. Always we must be on the look-out for real evidence from an impartial study of the numerical relations of all four combinations of success and failure with State management and private management. We must also remember that, in all such cases, real evidence can only come from the skilled researches of experts and not by any thinking or argumentation we can do for ourselves.

Social research of this kind is, of course, going on, and in time we shall know a lot more of the exact facts on which sound political and social decisions depend. It is still true that the total amount of such research is small compared with that done in the physical sciences. It still seems more important to those directing research funds that we should know about sub-atomic particles than that we should know about the behaviour of human beings. If we took seriously the ideal of making into an exact science the management of national and international affairs there would be a great deal more research in social psychology. Much of our expenditure on political orators and other means of influencing public opinion would be more profitably diverted to social research so that political action might be based on exact knowledge.

In the meantime, we have to make up our minds on such evidence as is available, and that, we know, is incomplete. This means that although we must make up our minds definitely we must not do so finally, but we must be willing to be guided by experience, being sure that experience will often lead us to change our minds on subjects about which we have felt most certain.

CHAPTER III

SOME DISHONEST TRICKS IN ARGUMENT

WE HAVE already noticed that a statement of the form 'All Xs are Y' is very rarely true and is very easily disproved. It is easily disproved for the obvious reason that a single instance of an X that is not Y is sufficient to overthrow it. If, for example, a man maintains that all pacifists are cowards, his opponent need point to only one pacifist who has shown courage by facing death bravely and his opponent's case is overthrown. If, on the other hand, his opponent had maintained the more moderate proposition that some pacifists are cowards, he could not have been defeated, for he could undoubtedly have brought forward one or more examples of pacifists who were cowards, and his contention would then be established.

This suggests that, in an argument, a man who maintains an extreme position (such as 'All Xs are Y') is in a very unfavourable position for successful controversy. Many people consciously or unconsciously adopt a trick based on this principle. This is the trick of driving their opponents to defend a more extreme position than is really necessary for their purpose. Against an incautious opponent this can often be done simply by contradicting his more moderate assertions until in the heat of controversy he boldly puts forward more and more extreme ones.

Let us suppose, for example, that two men are arguing about the conditions of some country under a Communist government. M maintains that the people are starving, that industry is hopelessly inefficient, and that the people are only kept from a successful counter-revolution by terror. N holds against him the more moderate position that things are not as bad as M paints them, and that in some respects the workers are better off than they are in some non-Communist countries. Clearly M is holding a position less easy to defend than the other, and we should expect the victory to go to N. So it probably would if N were content to stick to the very moderate set of propositions that he has laid down, which are really all that is needed to overthrow M. As the argument goes on, however, M makes exaggerated statements of the bad conditions of the workers in Communist countries, and, by a natural reaction, N makes equally wild statements of their prosperity, until he is maintaining a picture of universal well-being in these countries which his facts are quite insufficient to support. M now assumes the offensive and brings forward facts sufficient to overthrow the over-favourable view of the conditions in Communist countries which N has been incautious enough to defend, and N loses the argument. Yet he had a winning case to begin with. How often we see an adventurous controversialist wrecked in this way!

A person cautious in argument will not, however, be so easily led to court defeat. He will constantly reaffirm the moderate and defensible position with which he started, and the extreme statements of his opponent will be rebutted by evidence instead of leading him on to equally extreme statements on the other side. Against such a person, however, a similar trick is used very commonly in a more blatantly dishonest way. He has asserted moderately and truly that 'Some Xs are Y', but his opponent argues against the proposition that all Xs are Y. If he answers his opponent's arguments at all, he can only do so by defending the proposition 'All Xs are Y'. Then he has fallen into the trap. If he avoids this by reasserting his original position, his opponent often brings against him a particularly silly piece of sophistry which runs: 'But you ought logically to say that all Xs are Y if you think some Xs are Y'.

Let us call this device the 'extension' of one's opponent's statement. It can be used by luring him on to extend it himself in the heat of controversy, or, more impudently, by misrepresenting what he has said, or by the device of saying that 'he ought logically' to be defending the extended proposition. It is a device often used in argument, sometimes no doubt involuntarily; the remedy is always to refuse to accept an extension but to reaffirm the position which one really wants to defend.

An example of an attempt to force an extension on to a speaker comes from a time between the wars when there was considerable distress in Great Britain. The speaker argued that, with so much distress amongst the less well off, the country could not afford heavy expenditure on expensive luxuries, giving as an example the field sports of the rich. This was a moderate and reasonable proposition. One of his hearers accused him afterwards of inconsistency in attacking all expenditure on what were not necessities, since, presumably, the speaker had recreations of his own on which he expended money.

The speaker refused to have his proposition extended and reasserted his original statement that not all expenditure on recreation was undesirable, but that excessive expenditure was, pointing out that he had already shown that this was his view by arguing that some amount of luxury expenditure of this kind was desirable for everybody. His opponent now said: 'To be logically consistent, you ought to disapprove of all luxury expenditure if you disapprove of expenditure on grouse moors and deer forests'. To this unreasonable assertion I know of no satisfactory reply except to deny that there is any such logical necessity. The statement that 'Some luxury expenditure is socially undesirable' is as logically adequate as its extended substitute 'All luxury expenditure is socially undesirable' and seems more likely to be true. It would, of course, be reasonable and proper to ask the speaker by what criteria he distinguished between the kind of luxury expenditure that was socially undesirable and the kind of luxury expenditure that he considered to be desirable or at least harmless. One might also consider whether the reasons he gave for condemning field sports would also be reasons for condemning the speaker's own recreations. It is, however, not reasonable to misrepresent the speaker's contention that field sports were socially undesirable at that time by suggesting that he was condemning all luxury expenditure; that was a typical extension.

The use of the trick of the extension is common in controversy. There has been, for example, much discussion of the question of whether cricket or football teams should be admitted to our country for international matches from countries in which the members of the team are selected on grounds of race. That such teams should not be admitted because of the way in which they have been selected is an opinion held strongly by many people. An opponent of this opinion may, however, object that if teams from, let us say, South Africa are excluded because we disagree with the policy of separate racial development, we ought also to boycott teams from Russia, Portugal and other countries which adopt policies with which we disagree. This would be a reasonable objection if the suggested ground for exclusion of South African teams had been disagreement with the policy of separate development. If, however, the supporter of exclusion gave as his reason the fact of the racial selection of teams (which did not apply to the other countries mentioned), the reference to separate development is an extension of his proposition which he would be wise not to accept if what he wanted to defend was his original more limited statement.

In the same way, the defender of some social change may be met by the argument: 'You suppose that this piece of social reform will bring in the millennium.' The person attacked must reply: 'I don't suppose that it will bring in the millennium, or even that in itself it will solve all our more immediate problems. I only maintain that it will do something to reduce poverty by producing a more just distribution of wealth.' Clearly, if this is true, it is all that the speaker need maintain in order to convince his hearers that the reform is a desirable one. If he were led to make further claims, he would have fallen into the trap of the 'extension', and would find his proposition more difficult to defend. If he were foolish enough to walk so far into the trap as to maintain that his reform would bring about a perfect social order (implied by the word 'millennium'), his position would become impossible to defend.

Let us return to the attempt to force an extension by saying to one's opponent, 'Logically, you ought to believe that all luxury expenditure is socially undesirable if you think that expenditure on grouse moors and deer forests is socially undesirable.' This is an example of a debating trick which deserves special notice – the trick of using a sophistical formula in order to try to force a victory in argument. This particular one is not uncommon. If a pacifist argues that it is wrong to take part in a war, he may be told that to be logically consistent he ought to refuse to use violence in any circumstances, even against a criminal who was attacking his wife. This could be a sound argument and not a dishonest trick on one condition, that the pacifist defended his objection to war on grounds that would equally apply to the situation of his wife being attacked. If, however, (as is most likely to be the case) his reasons for not taking part in a war are not reasons for not protecting his wife from attack, the charge of logical inconsistency is merely a dishonest debating trick.

Another sophistical formula that is never an honest argument is the common use of the phrase 'the exception proves the rule'. When a man maintains an extreme position such as that members of the black-skinned races are incapable of intellectual development, he can quite properly be refuted by his opponent pointing to intellectually distinguished black men such as Booker Washington, Dr Bunche, and Professor Matthews. He may then try to justify his original extreme statement by saying: 'These are the exceptions that prove the rule.'

This is obviously a dishonest evasion. It can be dealt with by pointing out (as is self-evident) that exceptions do not prove that a general rule is true but that it is false. His opponent may also point out that the word 'prove' in this old saying originally had the meaning 'test', and that it is true that the way to test a general rule is to look for exceptions to it, whereas it is obviously not the case that finding exceptions 'proves' the rule in the modern sense of showing that the rule is a correct one.

Another common trick in controversy is that of the 'diversion'. This is the defence of a proposition by stating another proposition which is not a proof of the first one but which diverts the discussion to another question, generally to one about which the person who makes the diversion feels more certain. One man may say, for example, that the laws in South Africa on apartheid are oppressive to the black population. His antagonist replies that this is nonsense because the South African Government spends a great deal of money on the housing of Africans. The second statement may be true but it is not relevant to the first one since obviously the second speaker would not maintain that a country in which much money is spent on the housing of a part of its population cannot be a country in which that part of its population is oppressed by the laws. That some laws are oppressive to part of a population and that money is spent on the housing of that part of the population are two different statements. Either or both of them may be true or false, and the truth or falsity of one implies nothing about the falsity or truth of the other.

This is a diversion because the speaker has shifted the discussion from one topic to another under the appearance of producing an argument for the original topic. Such diversions are found very commonly in arguments; sometimes they are deliberate and sometimes they are unintended. Examples of the use of the diversion can be found in the correspondence columns of our newspapers. Nearly every controversy that is started is not carried to a conclusion because one side or the other creates a diversion in the third or fourth letter. A discussion of the claims of the Roman Catholic Church may, for example, degenerate in the course of half a dozen letters into an acrimonious squabble about the sale of indulgences in mediaeval England or about the social condition of the Papal States at the beginning of the last century. Still more often it degenerates into a discussion as to which of the two disputants is the more reliable historian, or shows the greater respect for 'logic'. Indeed, diversions from any argument to a dicussion of the personal characteristics of the disputants are so common as probably to form the majority amongst diversions. Many disputes end in this way even when they begin with a purely factual problem (such, for example, as which of two motorcars was on the wrong side of the road).

Into the class of diversions we must put too the trick of fastening on a trivial point in an opponent's argument, defeating him on that, and then leaving it to be supposed that he has been defeated on the main question. A man bringing forward a large number of facts in support of a contention may very well bring forward one, at least, that is not correct. The incorrectness of that fact may not be enough to undermine his conclusion, but an opponent who fastens on that one fact and proves its wrongness can easily create the impression that the whole position of the other is discredited although, in fact, the main support of the argument remains firm. A spurious victory has been gained by a successful diversion. In this case the diversion has not been, as in earlier examples, to a new question but to a side issue in the question under discussion.

An example of diversion to a side issue is to be found in the discussion given in the appendix to this book where the Professor maintains that Nature effects all improvements in races of animals by a process of elimination of the unfit by natural selection, giving as examples the strength of the horse and the swiftness of the greyhound. The Clergyman makes the true but somewhat trivial objection that the swiftness of the greyhound is the result of breeding and not of natural selection. This, however, is a side issue since there are plenty of other examples that the Professor might have chosen; he does, in fact substitute the wolf for the greyhound and his main argument is in no way discredited by the Clergyman's objection.

There is indeed a danger that any reference to the crooked thinking in an argument may be a diversion from a proper consideration of whether the conclusion of the argument is true or false. A true conclusion, as well as a false one, may be supported by crooked arguments. This does not relieve us of the necessity for examining the arguments to see whether they are sound or not. This is necessary as a preliminary step towards making a judgement as to whether the conclusion of the argument is true or not. But it is only a preliminary; if it is allowed to take the place of a consideration of the truth of the conclusion that is being argued about, it becomes a diversion.

A more impudent form of the same trick is diversion by the use of an 'irrelevant objection'. This is by denial of a fact brought forward by a disputant when the truth of this fact is of no importance at all (and not merely of minor importance) to the main argument.

A common way in which it is used is to fasten on some minor detail of one's opponent's case in which he is misinformed. A man may say, for example, that the doctrine of the Divine right of kings was overthrown in 1648 by the beheading of Charles I. His opponent points out that Charles I was beheaded in 1649 and not 1648. This is true, but has no bearing on the argument. A man arguing against the verbal accuracy of the Bible says that he does not believe that Jonah was swallowed by a whale. His opponent points out what is said in the Bible is that Jonah was swallowed by a great fish and that the whale is not a fish. Again true, but irrelevant, since presumably the speaker would find equal difficulty in believing this.

Of course, one ought to be accurate in detail so that one is not open to this kind of irrelevant objection. But we all make mistakes sometimes, and this way of making use of one's opponent's mistakes is dishonest argumentation.

Although the weakness of the irrelevant objection is obvious if one thinks about it, this trick is often successfully employed. It is particularly likely to be successful if the objection is of a humorous character. Thus a speaker attacking shortage of housing may refer to a family of six living in a single room not large enough to swing a cat in. His opponent (or an interrupter) may say: 'Then they shouldn't keep a cat'. It is not a good joke, but it may be a successful diversion because the person against whom it is used is in danger of appearing somewhat ridiculous in his efforts to bring the discussion back to the point from which it is diverted. The audience are more willing to laugh with the person who made the diversion than to follow the laborious efforts of his opponent to return to seriousness. It is a mean way of trying to win a reputation for being clever, and the person who habitually makes humorous diversions in a serious argument deserves no sympathy.

An example of diversion by irrelevant objection occurred when Mr Gorton was Prime Minister of Australia. He was reported to have said on one occasion that a speech by the leader of the opposition was 'as full of falsehoods as a suet pudding is full of currants'. A newspaper correspondent said that he had consulted an authoritative cookery book and found that the recipe for suet pudding showed that it contained no currants. This can be defended as a joke against the Prime Minister who should not have been so careless as to confuse a suet pudding with a plum duff, but as a contribution to the discussion of whether the opposition leader's speech did or did not contain falsehoods, it must be ranked as a diversion by irrelevant objection.

The diversion can, of course, be used by the defender of a position as well as by the person who attacks it. When a man has made a statement and finds himself hard pressed in its defence, he may divert the discussion in a direction more in his favour by substituting for the original statement one that sounds like it but which is easier to defend. Some people habitually begin a discussion by stating an extreme position and then, when this is attacked, they substitute for it a more moderate statement. They thus gain a double advantage. By the original statement they challenge attention and gain an undeserved reputation for being bold thinkers, while the later diversion enables them to escape the crushing defeat in argument which they would otherwise suffer. It is easy for the onlookers to be led to suppose that the original extreme statement is the one that has been successfully defended.

The remedy for all cases of diversion is to bring the discussion back to the question from which it started. This is not, in practice, always an easy thing to do, since an unscrupulous debater will then object that you are evading his arguments.

With care and good temper, however, it can generally be done.

There is a device related to diversion which we may mention here. That is the trick of bringing in defence of a statement another statement which does not in fact prove it, trusting that one's opponent will not challenge the proof. This can often be ensured by making the supporting statement a reference to a learned theory of which one's opponent will be afraid to confess his ignorance, or, at any rate, making the supporting statement in a matter so obscure that one's opponent fears that it would show shameful ignorance if he confessed that he did not see the connection.

I have heard, for example, democratic government opposed on the ground that it contradicts 'biological principles', and the raising of wages on the ground that 'wealth cannot be divided into parts'. Let us call this method that of the 'inconsequent argument'. The form of the inconsequent argument is simply 'A must be true because of B', when, in fact, A does not follow from B at all. For example, during the 1939–1945 war I heard a propaganda broadcast from Germany in which it was said that Mr Churchill was First Lord of the Admiralty in the 1914–1918 war, and was again occupying the same post in 1939, and that this proved that the war was made by Mr Churchill. This is a completely inconsequent argument, for there is no logical connection between the premisses and the conclusion. It is not even to be regarded as a fallacious reasoning process; it is, indeed, not a reasoning process but a verbal device for creating conviction in those willing to be convinced. It is as inconsequent as if I said: 'My neighbour's dog is standing at his house door now and he was standing there yesterday morning, which proves that he stole the sausages from my larder yesterday afternoon.' Of course, the conclusion might be true, but the argument does nothing to prove that it is true.

The argument discussed on p 44 that the African population of South Africa cannot be oppressed by the apartheid laws because the South African Government spends money on African housing might be classified as an inconsequent argument. An inconsequent argument becomes the starting point of a diversion if it leads the discussion away from the original question to a consideration of the new point that has been brought forward, here the amount of money spent in South Africa on African housing. If, however, the new point does not lead to a new direction of discussion but the new point is treated as a proof of the original position, there is no diversion; it remains an inconsequent argument.

A completely inconsequent argument is perhaps not often used deliberately. It is rather that those engaged in discussion, when strongly convinced of the position they are defending, are inclined to be careless about the arguments they use in its favour. Inconsequent arguments are fairly common. If an opponent in argument is guilty of one, the remedy is to ask him to explain to you exactly how his argument proves his conclusion. This is to admit ignorance, and if the argument is not really inconsequent and your opponent can clearly show the connection, he will gain an advantage. If not, however, your confession of ignorance has done you no harm. Too much fear of admitting ignorance lays you open to much crookedness in argument.

Another dishonest argument is one mentioned by Bentham in his book *The Theory of Fictions*. It is still used fairly commonly. Its general form is to discourage action against some admitted evil by pointing to some other evil which is stated to be worse than the first evil, but about which the user of the argument is making no proposal to do anything. For example, as an argument against attempts to abolish war, it has been pointed out that more deaths have resulted from road accidents in this country during some number of past years than the total casualties of the Vietnam war. This would be a reasonable ground for regarding it as important to find out ways of reducing the number of road accidents, but it is a dishonest argument when it is urged as a reason for not trying to bring to an end the Vietnam war or whatever war we or our allies may be engaged in at any particular time.

The dishonesty of this argument lies in the fact that there is no good reason why we should not try to do both: to prevent people from being killed on the roads and also to prevent them from being killed in wars.

It is a useful argument for the dishonest debater because it is adaptable to a large number of situations. It can be used as an argument against action for the abolition of any evil, for there is no evil so bad that a worse one cannot be found to compare it with. Thus the debater may ask why radical politicians concern themselves with such trivialities as wages and social services in our own country when there is the terrible threat of world over-population endangering the very foundation of our civilization. In time of war, motorists who are brought into the courts for exceeding the speed limit or for parking offences argue that the police should not be concerning themselves with such minor matters when all energy should be directed to the one important end of winning the war. When there was controversy in Australia as to whether racially segregated sporting teams from South Africa should play matches in Australia, some of those in favour of their admission argued that those opposing the South African teams were hypocritical because Australian neglect of its aboriginal population was worse than the South African treatment of its African population – a sound argument for improving the treatment of Australian aborigines but not for refraining from protest against racial segregation in sporting teams if one thinks that such segregation is wrong. These may all be considered to be clever debating tricks but quite unsound when judged as rational arguments. The reply to all of them is that if Y is a worse evil than X, this is no reason for not trying to remove X although it is a sound reason for fighting even more energetically against Y.

Lastly there is a common trick of argument which seems not generally to be recognized as a trick, so it seems worthwhile to discuss it here. It is the device of presenting one's own view as the mean between two extremes. We all love a compromise, and when someone recommends a position to us as an intermediate one between two extreme positions, we feel a strong tendency to accept it. Knowing this, people of the most diverse opinions present their views to us in this way.

A Liberal canvasser comes to us and points out that the Conservatives represent one extreme in politics and that the Socialists represent the other, while the Liberal party steers a moderate course between these two extremes. We feel, as moderate men, that we must support the Liberal party. This faith is a little shaken when the Conservative canvasser calls and points out that the Conservative idea of constitutional liberty is midway between the radicalism of the progressive parties and the tyranny of fascism. We are still further shaken when the Labour canvasser urges us to support a party that steers a mean direction between the capitalist parties on the one hand and revolutionary Communism on the other. Finally perhaps, we find ourselves at a Communist meeting where the speaker points out (quite truly) that the Communist programme avoids on the one hand the extreme position of the capitalist parties and the bourgeois Socialists and, on the other hand, that of the anarchists who deny the necessity for any organized government at all.

By this time we should sadly have come to the conclusion that the idea that truth lies always in the mean position between two extremes is of no practical use as a criterion for discovering where the truth lies, because every view can be represented as the mean between two extremes.

A second reason for distrusting this piece of crooked thinking is the fact that when we have two extreme positions and a middle one between them, the truth is just as likely to lie on one extreme as in the middle position. If I wished to convince you that two and two makes five, I might commend it to you as the safe middle position between the exaggerations on the one hand of the extremists who assert that two and two makes four, and on the other of those who hold the equally extreme view that two and two makes six. I should appeal to you as moderate men and women not to be led away by either of these extreme parties, but to follow with me the safe middle path of asserting that two and two makes five. As moderate men and women, perhaps you would believe me, but you and I would alike be wrong because the truth would lie with one of the extremes.

It is not, of course, to be supposed that every representation of a position as a mean between two extremes is necessarily a dishonest argument; it may not be an argument at all. It is a useful teaching device which may be used quite honestly as a means of explaining a position but not as a way to persuade one's hearers of its truth. If, for example, a lecturer on social psychology wants to explain how much of decent and social-ized behaviour in human beings is based on their inborn tendencies, he may contrast Hobbes's view that men are naturally at war with one another and are only kept good citizens by fear with that of Kropotkin who supposed that instinctively they were altruistic and only became self-seeking by the bad effects of the social organization under which they live in a capitalist society. He may point out objections to both of these views and then develop a middle view that there are both inborn tendencies to socialized behaviour and inborn anti-social (or criminal) tendencies. He need not say or suggest that this view is true because it is a mean between the views of Hobbes and Kropotkin; he may only have used these views as a help to making clear what his own position is. Any view can conveniently be explained by comparing it with other views, and it can best be explained by comparing it with two sets of views differing from it in opposite directions. It is, however, dangerously easy to slip from this honest use of comparison to the crooked thinking of suggesting that a position ought to be accepted because it is the mean between two extremes.

This is a trick so commonly used that many people do not recognize it as crooked thinking at all. It cannot, therefore, be dealt with effectively simply by pointing out that the trick is being used. It can, I think, best be rebutted by pointing out that other positions which would not be accepted by one's opponent (as, for example, the position one happens to be defending) can also be represented as a mean between two extremes.

CHAPTER IV

SOME LOGICAL FALLACIES

THE DEBATING tricks described in the preceding chapter, such as that of suggesting that a statement ought to be believed because it can be expressed as a mean between two extremes, are generally used in an open and undisguised form. There are other faults in reasoning which would be obvious to the most inefficient reasoner if they were displayed in a simple manner, but which may well be overlooked in the actual course of argument, where many of the steps are left out and the general structure of the argument is hidden under a multitude of words and made difficult to recognize by the fact that the argument is about something on which we feel strongly.

Whether the argument is really a sound one can then often be made clear if we tidy it up and reduce it to a skeleton form in which we replace the serious matter the argument is about by some trivial matter about which we do not feel strongly or by a mere set of symbols A, B, and C about which we have no feelings at all.

For example, suppose that we hear the following argument in a discussion of fascism: 'Any organization of society in which the citizens are not free to criticize the government is a bad one, whatever benefits of material prosperity and national unity it may bring its citizens. On this ground we must condemn the fascist system of government since in such countries, criticism of the government is treated as a crime.'

There are obviously two questions that may be asked about this argument: whether the facts asserted in it are correct, and whether the argument is a sound one in the sense that, if the facts were true, the conclusion would follow. We are here concerned only with the second of these questions, as to the soundness of the argument. As a step towards judging this, we may simplify the argument to the form:

> All governments that may not be criticized by their citizens are bad,
> A fascist government is one that may not be criticized by its citizens,
> Therefore, a fascist government is bad.

Or we may further simplify the argument by means of a set of symbols in which A stands for the class of governments whose citizens are not free to criticize them, B for the class of bad things, and C for the class of fascist governments. The argument is then reduced to the form:

> All As are Bs,
> All Cs are As,
> Therefore, all Cs are Bs.

which is the general structure of a class of familiar and obviously sound arguments.

In the language of the traditional Aristotelian logic, this is a syllogism in the mood of *Barbara*. It is clearly evident that the argument is a sound one: in other words, that if the first two of these statements (the premises) are correct, then the third (the conclusion) rigidly follows.

The soundness of the argument can be made even clearer if we represent the argument by a diagram in which the surface of the large outside circle represents B (the class of bad things), that of the smaller circle inside it represents A (the class of governments not allowing criticism by their citizens)

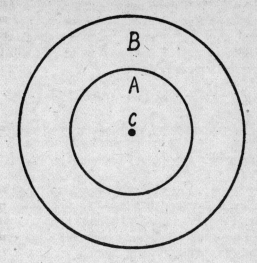

and the small black circle in the middle represents the class of fascist governments.

The situation stated in the argument that all governments of the A kind are bad is represented on the diagram by the circle A being wholly included within the circle B, and the situation that all fascist governments are of the A kind is shown by the small black circle C being wholly inside the circle A. It evidently follows that the C circle must be wholly inside B, that all fascist governments must be bad. Other controversialists might, of course, use this argument with a different C; instead of 'fascist government', it might be 'military dictatorship', or 'Communist government', or C might be the government of some particular country.

When we say that an argument is sound, we mean no more than that it is in a logically correct form, and that if the premisses are true the conclusion necessarily is also true. This obviously is not enough to ensure that the conclusion is true; we must also know that the statements contained in the premisses are correct. For example, we might construct such an argument as the following:

> *All fungi are poisonous,*
> *Mushrooms are fungi,*
> *Therefore, mushrooms are poisonous.*

This is a sound argument but, although it is correct in logical form, the first premiss is false. An argument of correct logical form based on false premisses can lead either to a true or to a false conclusion. We might have made the above argument lead to a true conclusion, while keeping the first false premiss by substituting 'death-caps' for 'mushrooms' in the second and third lines. The conclusion would now be true, death-caps are indeed poisonous. It is still the case, however, that the sound argument based on false premisses does not prove the conclusion: we cannot infer from it whether the conclusion is true or false, as we can from a sound argument with true premisses. It is a trick sometimes found in argument for those who are trying to get accepted false or doubtful facts as their premisses to draw attention to the formal logical correctness of their argument. They may indeed wind up their very dubious argument with the triumphant assertion 'And that's logic!'

If we cannot prove a conclusion by an argument which is correct in its logical form but is based on false premisses, it is also true that we cannot prove a conclusion by an unsound form of argument based on true premisses. Let us, for example, consider the following argument:

'The delusions which mislead men arise from their tendency to believe that to be true which corresponds to their wishes. One of the strong desires that affects human belief is the hope that man will escape extinction at death and live eternally in some ideal haven of bliss. No one who has any understanding of the origin of delusional systems in human wishes can fail to conclude that this belief in immortality is a delusion.'

Again, we may be uncertain whether or not this is a sound argument both because it deals with a matter on which we are inclined to feel strongly and also because the structure of the argument is concealed by a lot of words. But, if we reduce it to a simple form it becomes:

> *Delusions are beliefs in what we wish to be true,*
> *Belief in immortality is belief in what we wish to be true,*
> *Therefore, belief in immortality is a delusion.*

or, in an A, B, C symbolism:

> *All As are B,*
> *C is a B,*
> *Therefore, C is an A.*

That this argument is unsound is clear if we replace it by a trivial example with true premisses which leads to an obviously false conclusion:

> *All cats are four-legged animals,*
> *All dogs are four-legged animals,*
> *Therefore, all dogs are cats.*

The unsoundness of this form of argument becomes apparent if we try to draw for it a diagram like that on p 57. We should have to put the circle representing A inside the circle representing B, but all we should know about the dot representing C is that it must be somewhere inside the big circle B; it might be either inside or outside the smaller circle A. In other words, the conclusion might be true or false.

This particular form of crooked thinking is called by logicians 'the fallacy of the undistributed middle'. It has this name because the term common to both premisses, the 'middle term' B, does not cover the whole class (of beliefs in things we wish to be true) in either of the premisses. That is, in both premisses the word omitted before B is 'some' and not 'all'. It is plainly not the case that all beliefs in things that we wish to be true are delusions; some are and some are not. We wish when we go to bed to be alive and well when we wake up the next morning and most generally we are; we may also wish that we shall win a prize on a lottery ticket we hold and most generally we do not. If we believe that we are sure to win, that belief will be a delusion. If the first premiss in the above argument had been that all beliefs founded on what we wish to be true were delusions, the argument would be logically sound but its first premiss would be false. As has already been pointed out, a conclusion derived from an argument in correct logical form with false premisses is no more to be relied on than is a conclusion derived from faulty logic. The most that can properly be concluded from the facts put forward in this argument is that belief in immortality may be a delusion. If one wants to decide whether it is or not, it must be from other considerations than the fact that the belief coincides with our wishes.

Arguments of this type are not as uncommon as one might suppose. Naturally they are on matters on which feeling is strong, and generally they are not expressed in such a simple form that the process is apparent. But this kind of argument is found: 'The so-called moderate Socialists are only disguised Communists. They want to transfer industry from private hands to the State. That is what the Communists have done in Russia.' Or, alternatively, 'The capitalist governments of

Great Britain and the USA are fascist. The fascist government of Germany was anti-Communist, and so are the governments of Great Britain and the USA.' Both of these arguments and all others of the same type are examples of the fallacy of the undistributed middle.

It is perhaps most commonly met with as a part of the propaganda to discredit an individual who supports a cause not approved by the more conventional elements of public opinion, one, for example, who takes a leading part in opposition to a war in which his country is engaged. The propaganda against such an individual may take some such form as this: 'Dr S. is constantly criticizing the part played by our country in the present war. Opposition to the war is one of the planks of Communist propaganda. So it is evident that Dr S. is in reality a Communist.' Reduction of this argument to a skeleton form shows that it too is a fallacy of the same type. What is stated in the premises is not inconsistent with there also being non-Communist critics of the war, or with Dr S. being one of these. The conclusion 'that Dr S. is in reality a Communist' is, therefore, not proved.

The first step necessary to enable us to detect logical fallacies in argument is that we should get out of the habit of judging the soundness of an argument by considering whether we agree with its conclusion, and concentrate instead on examining its form. Since often the form is obscured by the way the argument is presented, and since also we are inclined to overlook unsoundness of form if the subject-matter of the argument is one on which we feel strongly, it is well to form the habit of putting arguments about which we are doubtful into a skeleton form with A B C symbolism. When we have done that we should be able to see at once whether the argument is sound or not. The main practical value of logic to one who wants to distinguish between straight and crooked thinking is that it introduces him to the device of reducing arguments to their skeleton form as a means of judging whether or not they give sound support to their conclusions.

The syllogism is an old form of skeleton argument and it is often convenient to use, but it is not the only one available. Let us consider another way of achieving the same end.

The beginning of every argument can be reduced to the form of a statement that if P is true of some particular X, then Q is also true of X. The argument given on p 55, for example, may be expressed in the form: If a government can't be criticized by its citizens, then that government is a bad one. P (that it can't be criticized by its citizens) is true of a fascist government, so it follows that Q (it is a bad one) is also true of a fascist government. Obviously the conclusion follows soundly from what goes before: if it is agreed that any government that can't be criticized by its citizens is a bad one, and that a fascist government can't be criticized by its citizens, then it cannot be denied that a fascist government is bad.

Another conclusion that can legitimately be drawn from 'If P, then Q' is that for any particular for which Q is false, P also must be false; if the government of any country is a good one, it must be the case that the government of that country is one that allows criticism of itself by its citizens.

In other words. From the fact that if P is true then Q is true (that P implies Q), we can draw two sound conclusions:

(1) That for anything of which P is true, Q must also be true.

(2) That for anything of which Q is false, P must also be false.

There are also two fallacious conclusions that might erroneously be drawn from the fact that if P is true, then Q is true. These are:

(1′) That for anything of which Q is true, P must also be true. From knowing that the government of a country was a bad one, we could not conclude that its citizens were not free to criticize it; other features of a government may make it bad as well as restrictions on its citizens' freedom to criticize it.

(2′) That for anything for which P is false, Q must also be false. Knowing its citizens were free to criticize the government, we could not safely conclude that the government was a good one; it might be or it might not be.

When we say that the last two conclusions are fallacious, we do not mean that they are necessarily false, only that their truth does not follow from what has gone before; they may be true or false. That they are fallacious is perhaps best made clear by a simple example in which the conclusion is obviously false. There is no doubt that being an elephant implies having a trunk. To infer from this that any animal with a trunk must be an elephant would be a fallacy of the type 1′. The conclusion is obviously wrong since a tapir also has a trunk. To infer from the above statement that any animal not an elephant has no trunk would be a fallacy of type 2′; it also is refuted by the fact that the tapir has a trunk.

At this level of simplicity of material this may all seem self-evident. It may be by no means self-evident in the more complicated kinds of argument in which these fallacies do actually occur. For dealing with these more complicated arguments, the method of reduction to a skeleton form is a useful testing tool. The argument, for example, that Dr S. must be a Communist because he opposes a war which the Communists also oppose can be reduced to the form of the fallacious argument 2′: if P implies Q, then Q implies P. In this case:

Being a Communist implies opposition to the war,
So opposition to the war implies being a Communist.

The conclusion that Dr S. must be a Communist because he is opposed to the war no more necessarily follows than does the conclusion that the tapir is an elephant. The other examples given to illustrate the fallacy of the undistributed middle may also be treated in this way.

There is thus more than one way of reducing an argument to a form in which its soundness or unsoundness becomes apparent. We can use either or both of the methods described. Our choice will be determined by the practical convenience of choosing the way which best serves the purpose of making clear to ourselves and to those we have discussions with, which of the arguments we or they use are sound and which unsound.

I should not wish the above discussion of logical forms to lead readers to buy an elementary textbook on logic and start learning by heart the sound and unsound forms of the syllogism. That might be a useful activity for the purpose of passing an examination in logic, but not for our present purpose of learning to detect and avoid mistakes in reasoning. What is to be learnt from logic for this purpose is, I would suggest, its techniques of reducing arguments to a skeleton form. When this has been done, we should be able to see directly whether the arguments are sound or not. If we are still in doubt, we can try various subject matters for the arguments and see whether they lead invariably to true conclusions. If they sometimes lead to true conclusions and sometimes to false, the form of the arguments must be unsound.

Before ending this chapter it may be well to mention two fallacious arguments which are known to every schoolboy – the argument in a circle and the argument which begs the question about which the dispute is taking place. These are somewhat less common in adult controversy than the fallacies which have been already mentioned, but they are found sufficiently often to be worth a short examination.

The general form of the argument in a circle is: 'P is true because of Q; Q is true because of P'. It is sometimes argued for example, that human action is not free because what happens in a choice between two actions (let us say, between running away and standing one's ground in danger) is that the stronger impulse (to stand one's ground, for example) overcomes the other. If we further ask how we know that the impulse to stand one's ground was the stronger, the reply is that it must be so because that is the behaviour which actually took place. The argument then reduces to the form: the impulse to stand still overcame the impulse to run away because it was the stronger impulse; it was the stronger impulse because it overcame the other – an entirely circular argument.

We have already (in Chapter I) mentioned the crooked argument by 'begging the question' or assuming what is to be proved. This cannot be done blatantly: if one began an argument by stating as an agreed principle the point that was in dispute, the trick would be too transparent to be successful. It can, however, be done by using a form of words which implies the conclusion, although not in an obvious way. The example given in Chapter I of the use of words involving moral judgements when a moral question is at issue is a fairly transparent trick, but it is not uncommon as an important part of a complicated argument. If a disputant wants to establish the guilt of an individual or a group of men, he is likely to use an argument in which he describes them as 'scoundrels', 'unprincipled blackguards', etc.

Another method of using the same trick is to assume what has to be proved in a definition. In order that this trick may be used, it is not necessary that formal definition of the words used should take place. The question-begging definition may only be implied.

Let us suppose that A and B dispute as to whether Christians lead better lives than those who are not Christians. A maintains that they do, but in opposition to him B points to numerous persons who go to church and profess Christian beliefs but who drink too much, neglect their families, and lead otherwise discreditable lives. A, however, refuses to accept this as evidence against his contention on the ground that those who do such things are not 'really' Christians. A's argument implies a definition of Christians which includes as one of the essential marks the leading of a virtuous life. The question in dispute is begged by the definition of a Christian which is implied by A.

Clearly one can prove a large number of propositions by a similar method. One could prove that all swans are white by refusing to count as a swan any bird that was not white. Some people are unwilling to admit that this is a crooked argument. They may argue that the word 'Christian' is used in various ways and that a definition which includes the leading of a virtuous life as one of the essential marks of a Christian is not unusual and quite legitimate, and if the definition be accepted, then the conclusion cannot be denied. This is true, and if the statement that all Christians lead virtuous lives is taken simply as a statement of how we are going to use the word 'Christian', no important objection can be made against it. In the argument given above, however, A meant more than a statement about how he used words: he certainly meant to state a proposition about outside fact. This proposition was that those who possessed the external marks of being Christians (going to church, professing the Christian creed, etc) also tended to possess the character of leading a virtuous life. This may well be true, but it cannot be established by the argument which A used, for he begged the question at issue by his definition.

Argument in a circle and begging the question are universally recognized as dishonest tricks in argument. In order to refute an opponent who uses one of them, it is therefore only necessary to show that the trick is being used. In order to do this it is sometimes necessary to put one's opponent's arguments in a simpler form so that the error may be more easily seen. Particularly is this the case when the question has been begged by choice of words or by definition.

CHAPTER V

WORDS AND FACTS

IN ONE of his books, the American psychologist and philosopher William James tells a story of how, during a camping holiday, he returned from a solitary walk to find the rest of the camping party engaged in a ferocious philosophical dispute. The problem was this. Suppose that a squirrel is on one side of a tree-trunk and a man on the other side. The man starts going round the tree, but however fast he goes round, the squirrel goes round in the same direction, so that he keeps the trunk of the tree between the man and himself. The philosophical question was as to whether the man went round the squirrel or not. The disputants were evenly divided, and it is not surprising to learn that they had disputed for a long time without coming any nearer to a solution of the problem. They appealed to James, who replied that it was not a question of facts but of words, of how one is to use the words 'go round'.

This is a trivial example of a very important type of dispute, in which the question at issue cannot be determined because both sides treat as a problem of fact what is really a problem of words. Clearly no question of fact divided the disputants. Those who said that the man went round the squirrel pointed out that he was first to the north of the squirrel, then to the west of it, then to the south, then to the north again. But this fact was not disputed by their opponents. Those who said the man did not go round the squirrel pointed out that he was not successively to the front of it, then to the side of it, then to the back of it, etc. Again this fact was not disputed by the other side. Indeed, no question of fact divided them. The only question between them was the question of which of these sets of facts should be described by the words 'go round'. This particular verbal question could not be settled if they went on disputing for ever. Plainly it could not, in this case, be settled by an appeal to a dictionary, since no dictionary would be found to define 'going round' so precisely as to distinguish between these two possible uses of the words. Nor could it be settled by argument, since one has a perfect right to use the word 'going round' in whichever of the two ways one likes. If indeed the disputants had realized that their difference was a purely verbal one they would have stopped arguing, since they would have realized that it could not be settled. The important character of the dispute was that it was a verbal problem discussed as if it were a factual one.

Many discussions are of this type, and it is failure to realize their verbal nature that leads to much fruitless discussion of them. Perhaps when we were children we may have found ourselves involved in a dispute as to whether rhubarb is a fruit. Obviously no question of fact was involved; the question was the verbal one of how one is to use the word 'fruit'. If we follow the botanists in defining it as the part of a plant which encloses the seed, rhubarb is obviously not fruit but a stalk. If, however, we define 'fruit' as a vegetable growth that you cook with sugar for the sweet course of a meal, then rhubarb is a fruit. You have a right to use the word 'fruit' in either way. If the botanist insists that his is the one right way of using the word, you may point out that the other is also a present-day use; it may indeed be an older use. No one would, however, be much interested in arguing the question if they realized that it was only a question of how a word was to be used; what gave liveliness to the discussion was the mistaken idea that it was a dispute about a question of fact.

When we grow older, we may become students of philosophy and allow ourselves to be entrapped in the same kind of dispute when we discuss whether the colour green is in the outside world or in our own minds. If it is realized that this is only a verbal question of whether we are to use the word 'green' for the colour of grass and leaves or for the experience we have when we look at grass or leaves, it is clear that there is nothing interesting to discuss. We can use the word in either way; it is used in both ways in common speech, as when we say, 'The grass really is green, although it doesn't look green in this light', using 'green' for a property of the object the first time we use it and for a character of our experience the second time. We may use the word 'green' in either way, but when we want to think precisely about vision, we must not confuse the two uses. We can then distinguish these uses by adopting a new verbal convention, perhaps talking of 'object-green' when we mean the green of grass and leaves and of 'phenomenal green' when we mean the green of our visual experience. But for everyday communication, this would be an unnecessary complication; in ordinary life, we can use the word 'green' in both senses without misunderstanding one another.

Serious misunderstandings do, however, arise in other contexts by differences in the use of words being mistaken for differences of opinion about matters of fact. We may, for example, find three people of different religious denominations arguing about the Catholic Church. One says that the Catholic Church is the body of all the Christians who have bishops whose consecration has been in direct descent from the Apostles. Another says that the Catholic Church is the body of all Christians who are in communion with the Bishop of Rome. A third says that the Catholic Church is the whole body of Christian believers. Here is a dispute that can go on interminably, since it seems to the disputants to be a question of fact as to what is the Catholic Church. Probably none of the three would welcome the intervention of an onlooker who pointed out that the question which divided them was primarily a verbal one as to how the term 'Catholic Church' was to be defined. If you define it as the body of all Christians whose bishops are in the Apostolic succession, the first man would be right; if you define it as the body of all Christians in communion with the Bishop of Rome, the second man would be right; if as the body of all Christians, the third man would be right. But, whichever way you defined it, no question of fact would be altered, only the way in which a word was used. All three classes of Christians exist and all require naming if we are to talk about them. To avoid confusion, they had better be called by different names, but no necessity compels one to use one name rather than another for any of the three.

One reason why none of the disputants would welcome such a solution of their difference would be that they would all feel that nevertheless there was a real difference between them that was not verbal. Of course there is, but the real difference is only obscured by the confusion between fact and word that is made by their discussion of their difference as if it were the question of what the Catholic Church is. The real difference is one of moral valuation. It can be stated as: 'Ought one to belong to the body of Christians whose bishops have the Apostolic succession?', 'Ought one to belong to the body of Christians in communion with the Bishop of Rome?', etc.

This is a real difference and not one merely about the use of words, but, like most discussions involving the word 'ought', it is not one that it is very hopeful to try to settle by the method of argumentation. Probably if they realized that this was what divided them, they would stop arguing and agree to differ. It was the illusion of having a factual question as to the nature of the Catholic Church to settle that encouraged them to argue in the hope that some consideration of fact might settle it. The trouble here is not quite so simple as that of a merely verbal question discussed as if it were a factual one. It is a problem partly verbal and partly non-verbal in which it is necessary to disentangle the verbal and non-verbal elements before one can see clearly what the difference is about.

The confusion between verbal and factual problems or between verbal and factual elements in the same problem may not be dishonest argumentation; it may be lack of skill in the use of language that leads to such confusion. The confusion itself is very common. Such questions as: 'What is the real essence of democracy?', 'What is the nature of freedom?', 'What is instinct?' are all problems in which one is liable to find oneself disputing about questions of words as if they were questions of fact. In all of them the remedy is the same: to see what part of the difference is merely a difference in the use of words and then to see what difference (if any) remains as to fact or to valuation. I mean by 'valuation' such questions as to whether a thing is bad or good, beautiful or ugly. I think that we shall agree that such differences are not merely verbal differences, although they are differences which are difficult (perhaps impossible) to settle by argument.

There is a method of trying to use a verbal proposition to settle a question of fact which is perhaps worth noticing. Let us suppose that A and B are arguing about the merits of different kinds of education. A is a supporter of the old-fashioned type of discipline in schools, while B supports the more modern type of school in which the children are allowed a great deal of freedom. At some stage of the argument A says: 'You will admit that too much freedom in schools is a bad thing'. B feels at something of a disadvantage. He is asked to admit a proposition which seems damaging to his case, and yet he realizes that it is a proposition he cannot reasonably deny. He cannot deny it because it is purely a verbal proposition, since it says nothing factual at all. The meaning of 'too much' is 'a quantity so great that it is a bad thing'. It is indeed a tautology, that is, a verbal statement of the form 'X is X', and while a tautology cannot reasonably be denied, it also cannot be used to prove any fact. Of course, B might be willing to deny the implication of A's statement that there was any quantity of freedom in schools which was too great. Then he might justly accuse A of making an assertion whose implications begged the question at issue. Even so he would not be denying A's statement (which indeed cannot be denied); he would only be denying that it referred to any possible degree of freedom.

It is likely, however, that he is unwilling to defend such an extreme position as this. He is only prepared to argue that there should be a good deal more freedom in schools than A would allow. He will point out the tautological nature of A's statement in some such way as: 'Of course, too much of anything is a bad thing'. Then he will bring back the discussion to the real point at issue, saying perhaps: 'But what I should consider the right amount of freedom is what you would call "too much"'. Even so, if the discussion took place before a not very intelligent audience, A might most unfairly have been supposed to have scored a point.

Let us pause at this point to make clear the use of a convention that is generally adopted and which is very useful for avoiding confusion between facts and words. It is that of enclosing a word between single inverted commas when we are referring to the word itself and omitting the commas when we are talking about the thing the word stands for. Thus a verbal dispute will be about 'democracy', while a factual dispute may be about democracy, that is, about the systems of government for which the word 'democracy' stands. If we think we are discussing democracy when the question at issue is really about 'democracy', then we are mistaking a verbal for a factual dispute.

We can consider how verbal problems arise and how they come to be mistaken for factual problems in another way.

Suppose that someone said that he was going to use the symbol '9' for the first number, '8' for the next number, '7' for the number after that, and '2' for the number after that. It would be no good telling him that this was wrong; he would reply that he was living in a free country and could use symbols as he liked. Some of the arithmetical statements he would make would look very odd, such as that '8 times 8 is 2'. We might at first suppose that he has produced a new and extraordinary arithmetic. But this would be wrong: it would be the old arithmetic expressed in a new system of symbols. What he meant by '8 times 8 is 2' would be exactly the same as we meant by '2 times 2 is 4'. He would as it were, have made the same factual assertion in a new language. There would be obvious objections to what was proposed; it would serve no useful purpose and it would be inconvenient. Its adoption would not enable us to say anything new, and it would lead to much misunderstanding.

Of course, there might be a point in the use of a new symbolism. Mathematicians do sometimes use the symbol '10' for the number after 1, '11' for the next number, '100' for the next number, and so on. This is called expressing the numbers in 'the scale of 2'. Then the mathematician might say '11 times 11 is 1001', meaning exactly the same as we mean by '3 times 3 is 9'. This symbolism is convenient for some purposes, as, for example, for using with computers, but it does not enable the mathematician to say anything new, and, if he used this notation in a context in which the ordinary number symbols would be expected, he would have to explain the kind of number symbolism he was using if he wanted not to be misunderstood.

This may all seem obvious when we are talking about numbers; it is often overlooked when similar situations occur in the use of words. Suppose someone says: 'Democracy is not government by the people, but the willing agreement of the people with a system of laws imposed on them by their rulers', or 'Religion is not faith in God, but a sense of unity with the evolutionary process'. He is not, as the form of words might suggest, announcing some new and previously unknown fact about democracy or about religion; he is simply telling us that he is going to use the word 'democracy' or the word 'religion' in a way different from that of other people or perhaps simply different from that of his opponent.

There may be some point in his wish to use the word in a different way but, whether there is or not, endless confusion can result from failure to realize that that is what he is doing. He will use sentences different from those of his opponent when they are both saying the same thing. He may say, for example, 'Germany under Hitler was a true democracy' while his opponent may say, 'Hitler destroyed democracy in Germany' and there may be no difference of fact between these two statements, any more than there is between '3 times 3 is 9' in the ordinary use of numbers and '11 times 11 is 1001' when we are using the scale of 2. This is obviously the case when we consider that 'Germany under Hitler was a country in which there was willing agreement of the people with laws imposed on them by their rulers' is in no way inconsistent with the statement that 'Hitler destroyed government by the people in Germany'. They are different statements both of which may be true. They only appear to contradict one another when they are made with the word 'democracy' used with one meaning in one of them and with another meaning in the other.

To dispute about which of the two is the true statement without noticing that the difference is one in the use of words, is another example of mistaking a verbal difference for a factual one. Of course, the man who makes these statements about democracy being willing agreement of people with laws imposed on them or about religion being a sense of unity with the evolutionary process is very likely to invite this confusion by regarding himself as making a statement of fact and not an announcement of how he is going to use words. He may indeed make this confusion inevitable by claiming to have discovered the fact he thinks he is announcing. He may say, for example, that as a result of the study of Roman history or by having paid a visit to Russia he has learned that democracy is really the willing agreement of the people with laws imposed on them from above. Or he may say that by studying biology, or by staying in a Zen Buddhist monastery, he has discovered that religion is a sense of unity with the evolutionary process. This is nonsense. No study of non-verbal facts can tell him how to use a word. His studies and visits may convince him that the agreement of people with laws imposed on them is an important thing and, therefore, one that we should distinguish in words. They may convince him that it is a better thing than people making laws for themselves. But they cannot possibly tell him that the word 'democracy' has to be used for it. That is his own choice; he may bring arguments in its favour, but he cannot claim that the choice was forced on him by the facts.

The next stage of the dispute is likely to be the somewhat unprofitable one of whether these are the right uses of the words 'democracy' and 'religion'. His opponent may say, "Of course, you can use words in your own way and we will try to understand you, but what 'democracy' really means is government by the people." This is better than discussing 'what democracy really is', because it puts the difference at the right point, as a difference about the use of a word, not as a difference about a fact.

Yet it is not a very profitable thing to discuss. Not because there is no question as to the right use of a word, but because there are several different questions, all fairly easy to decide if they are separated out, but likely to lead to interminable disputes if they are confused together under the one question of the right use of the word.

The first question is what was the original meaning of the

word. Very often the words we are likely to dispute about have Greek, Latin, or Anglo-Saxon originals, and a good etymological dictionary will tell us what these are and what they meant. We learn, for example, that 'democracy' comes from the Greek *demos*, meaning 'people', and *krateo*, meaning the verb 'rule'. So its etymological meaning is 'rule by the people'. If we try 'religion', we find that this is derived from Latin *re*, meaning 'back', and *ligo*, meaning 'to bind'. If the etymological meaning of 'religion' is 'to bind back', this helps us very little in deciding which of the disputants is right in his use of the word 'religion'.

When people are disputing about the right use of a word, they are not likely to appeal to an etymological dictionary, which tells them about its Greek or Latin origin. They are more likely to claim that their sense of the word is the one in which it is ordinarily used. This certainly is a more important question. The ways in which words are used change in the course of time, and the origins of words are not always indications of how they are used now. The question as to how a word is used now is more important than that of what was its original meaning, but it is much less easy to decide. It may seem that we can turn to a dictionary to find out how a word is used now, but the kind of words we are likely to be disputing about, such as 'democracy' and 'religion', are used in many different ways. The better the dictionary, the more uses of a word it will give. The *Oxford English Dictionary* lists four main meanings of the word 'democracy' and eight main meanings of the word 'religion', and that falls far short of the real variety of their meanings. I should guess that if one examined various writers, it would not be difficult to find twenty different ways in which 'democracy' is used and forty in which 'religion' is used. So if someone says he wants to use either word in a new way, he is only increasing a diversity which was large before.

We cannot reasonably try to stop him from using these words in a new way by urging that they have a single clearly defined meaning which it would be wrong to depart from; this is very often not the case. If, however, the meaning he proposes is neither the original etymological meaning nor any of the currently accepted meanings, it is reasonable to point out that a new use adds to the confusion that already exists. But our complaint is rather that the new use is inconvenient than that it is wrong. If the person proposing the new use is willing to put up with the inconvenience of being very generally misunderstood, we need not waste time in trying to convince him that his use of the word is not the right one. What we must be clear about is that a new use of a word is not a new statement of fact. We must be clear that what we are differing about is a verbal problem and not a factual one.

During the present chapter we have been discussing those subjects of dispute that are factual and comparing them with those that are merely verbal. There is some danger of giving the impression that it is only the factual questions that are important and that questions of how to use words are not of any importance. That certainly would be a wrong idea. We want to avoid mistaking verbal questions for factual ones, but, when we have done that, we have the problem of how to deal with verbal questions as well as the problem of how to deal with factual ones. We can only hope to settle a question of fact by using observation or research to discover what really is the case. Then we have to use words to convey to other people what is the case as clearly and unambiguously as we can. This is obviously not unimportant, and it is not always very easy. Chapters VII and VIII will be particularly concerned with the solution of verbal problems; that is, with the skilful and unskilful use of words in thinking and communication.

CHAPTER VI

MISUSE OF SPECULATION

ANOTHER ERROR into which one can be led by failure to understand the relation of words to facts is that we may use speculative thinking to solve problems which can only be solved by the observation and interpretation of facts. In many of the questions which we want to decide it is very difficult to get an accurate and complete knowledge of the facts. So we are tempted to make our judgements without the necessary basis of fact. We may even be tempted to suppose that accurate thinking without the necessary facts will itself supply our needs.

Such *speculative thinking* has a certain legitimate use. By speculative thinking alone, man could have found out all the truths of pure mathematics. He could have discovered, for example, that 2 is the cube root of 8 and that 13 is a prime number. He could not, however, by mere speculation have advanced one step in any of the sciences. He could not have found out anything about human nature until he turned to the collection of facts about mankind, or about economics until he began to collect facts about such things as the production and distribution of goods.

The belief that one can find out something about real things by speculation alone is one of the most long-lived delusions in human thought. It is the spirit of anti-science which is always trying to lead men away from the study of reality to the spinning of fanciful theories out of their own minds. It is the spirit which every one of us (whether he is engaged in scientific investigation or in deciding how to use his vote in an election) must cast out of his own mind. Mastery of the art of thought is only the beginning of the task of understanding reality. Without the correct facts it will lead us into error.

We can distinguish as a special kind of crooked thinking the attempt to get knowledge of fact by speculative methods. This attempt is being made in any argument which tries to deduce what 'is' from what the speaker feels 'ought to be' or 'must be', or whenever a person in discussion tries to draw conclusions about facts from the use of words. Speculation has a legitimate place even in thought about external fact – that of suggesting new possibilities. We can properly use the speculative method to suggest what might be, but never to conclude what is. We can only draw conclusions as to facts by consideration of other facts.

Yet the illegitimate use of speculation is common. Our remedy is to examine on what grounds a conclusion as to fact is put forward. If these grounds are other facts, then the conclusion may or may not be a sound one. If the grounds are the speaker's conviction of what ought to be or what must be or the manner in which words are commonly used, then we must defeat our opponent's argument by showing that his conclusion is based on the kind of data from which no valid conclusion can be drawn.

While speculative thinking is by no means absent from discussions of practical affairs, it is particularly in those dealing with questions of a semi-philosophical order that this trick is prevalent: 'Man cannot have evolved from monkeys because the higher cannot be derived from the lower', or 'A vacuum cannot be produced because a space not occupied by matter is a contradiction', or 'Telepathy is not a possibility because a thought cannot pass from one mind to another without some physical means of communication.'

These are all speculative arguments; whether their conclusions are right or wrong, they cannot properly be asserted on the grounds given. In all such cases, we must examine the facts in order to discover whether the conclusions are true. Whether man is a product of evolution and, if so, from what forms he was evolved, are questions to be decided by evidence provided by the sciences of biology and geology. Whether a vacuum can be produced has been settled not by arguing about the problem but by successful attempts to pump out the air from an air-tight flask. Whether telepathy is possible is best determined by carrying out experiments between two people with no physical means of communication, and seeing whether, under such conditions, the thought of one can be influenced by the thought of the other. If our examination of the facts leads to a conclusion which we find to be inconceivable, this need not be regarded as telling us anything about the facts, but only about the limits of our powers of conceiving. We must learn to use our imaginations; we can conceive anything if we try hard enough.

The above speculative arguments are of the general form: 'So-and-so must be true because it is inconceivable that it should be otherwise.' There is another form of speculative argument which can be reduced to the form: 'So-and-so must be true because its truth is implied by the way we use language.'

For example, it was argued at one time that the soul was something independent of the body and that it must, therefore, survive the death of the body. The proper way of stating this argument would be that we use the word 'soul' as if it were a thing which existed apart from the body, and that this use of language disposes us to believe that it will survive the death of the body. It then becomes clear that it is a speculative argument based on our use of language. The conclusion, of course, may be true or false, but the argument itself gives no sound reason for asserting that the conclusion is true.

At the present time one is more likely to meet this argument used the other way round. It is said that such words as 'mind' or 'soul' are based on a mistake in the use of language. We know that we think, feel, etc, but it is a mistake in grammar to attribute these thinkings and feelings to a mind or soul. The idea that there might be something surviving bodily death is a mere result of this mistaken use of language, so there can be no survival of bodily death. This is equally a speculative argument of essentially the same type. It tries to draw a conclusion as to fact by the study of language.

In both cases the answer is that we must make our language fit the observed facts and not try to draw conclusions as to the facts from our use of language. If we are convinced that nothing survives the bodily death of a man, then we shall discard such a noun as 'soul' or 'spirit' from our vocabulary (unless, of course, we need it to cover some other fact). If, however, we think we have grounds for believing that man survives the death of his body, then we shall need some such noun as 'soul' or 'spirit' to stand for what survives. In either case our use of language must be determined by what appear to be the facts. We are making a misuse of speculation if we let our belief about facts be determined by our previous use of language.

It may be objected, however, that what is inconceivable cannot be true and that a self-contradictory statement cannot be true. There is a sense in which both of these propositions are true, but in that sense neither of them is of use as a means of discovering what is the case in the world around us, as distinct from the truths of pure mathematics or of logic. If someone says that man cannot have free-will because it is inconceivable that any action can take place without a preceding cause, it is necessary to ask in what sense it is inconceivable. Is it inconceivable in the sense that it is inconceivable that any even prime number greater than two should be found – because the supposition is intrinsically absurd? Then its inconceivability would be a sound reason for concluding that it was not the case. Or is it inconceivable in the sense that he finds it difficult to think of such a thing as an action not determined by a previous cause? Any such difficulty may simply be due to the limiting effects of his thought habits and not to any real impossibility. Non-Euclidean space is entirely inconceivable to most people, yet it apparently exists wherever there is a gravitational field. The ancient philosopher Zeno found motion inconceivable, yet he and other people managed to walk about. Modern physicists consider that some sub-atomic events are random and uncaused – an idea that would have been felt to be inconceivable by their fathers. Since we are continually extending the range of what we find we can conceive, we can obviously not accept the inconceivability of anything as a sufficient reason for supposing that it does not happen.

The question of contradictoriness as a criterion of truth is rather more difficult. If two statements contradict one another then one or both of them must be wrong. If a system of ideas is self-contradictory, then it cannot be right. The trouble is that what is wrong may not, however, be what we are trying to say, but the way we are saying it. Examination of ideas for self-consistency is a very valuable exercise when it is undertaken as a means of improving how we say things; it can be dangerous when it is taken to be a way of finding out whether what we are trying to say is true. A philosopher arguing with a simple man will generally succeed in showing him that the ideas he is trying to express are full of contradictions. The simple man may, however, protest: 'I can't express it consistently because I am not as clever as you, but what I am trying to say is right.' Most of us will sympathize with him. He is quite right not to give up his beliefs merely because the philosopher finds them self-contradictory. At the same time time, he would be wise to use the criticisms of the philosophers as a way of finding out how to say what he believes to be true without any inconsistencies.

When we say that speculative thinking is not a useful way of trying to find out what is true, we do not mean that it is of no use. It has already been suggested that the value of speculative thinking lies in its use for exploring possibilities as to what might be the case. What may be shutting us off from realizing the explanation of the facts around us is often that we have not thought of all the possibilities. Then what is needed in order that we may see a new truth may be the ability to speculate as to what might be. This ability to speculate may be an essential step towards new insights although it does not, in itself, tell us whether these new insights are or are not true.

Discoveries in science have often had to wait till someone had thought of a new possibility. When Newton considered that the force that made an apple fall to the ground was the same force as that which determined the movements of the heavenly bodies, he made a bold and fruitful speculation, the truth of which was shown by later researches. Darwin similarly speculated that evolution took place by the inheritance of differences in plants and animals which gave their possessors some advantage that made their survival more likely. He felt it necessary, however, to accumulate observations for another twenty years before he was convinced that his speculation was a true one.

A more recent example of this feature of scientific discovery is to be found in the work of Einstein, who was faced by certain contradictions in the physical sciences, particularly by the failure of experiment to find the expected difference in the velocity of light in different directions in a moving system. He tried out a new way of thinking about movement in which any such difference was no longer to be expected and within which the contradictions disappeared. So by speculative thought he developed the theory of relativity. This theory was not, however, merely a product of speculative thinking. The thinking was occasioned by a set of experimental observations, and the scientific world was only finally convinced that it was true when it was confirmed by another experimental observation, that the amount of deflection of light when it passed through a gravitational field was that predicted by relativity theory.

The type of thinking that enabled Newton, Darwin and Einstein to speculate so profitably is now generally called 'creative thinking' and it has attracted considerable recent attention from psychologists. Attempts have been made to devise tests to measure an individual's degree of creativity; these have not, so far, been very successful. The question has also been asked as to what extent our present methods of educating children, with their emphasis on giving the right answers, favour reproductive rather than creative thinking, and whether it would not be better to encourage children to explore new ways of thinking rather than training them to give the right answers. This is a question that may well be considered by all of those who are concerned with the education of children.

A recent writer on this subject is the Cambridge medical psychologist, de Bono. He uses the term *lateral thinking* for the ability to solve a problem not by pursuing a single line of thought, but by trying out a new one. He has devised ingenious exercises, both practical and verbal, which require lateral thinking for their solution.

I do not know whether doing Dr de Bono's exercises make one more ready to try new lines of thought in connection with politics, religion, or one's business. It may do so, and the possibility is well worth exploring. What de Bono is inviting his readers to do is essentially the same as what is done by a chess player or a solver of chess problems. Both have to look for a promising line of action and when this is tried out and found not to work, they must turn their back on this line and try something different. The good player or problem-solver is using lateral thinking in this context. It may be that this also makes it more possible for him to try out new lines of thought in the problems of everyday life, although it is by no means certain that it does so.

In such triumphs of creative thinking as Newton's theory of gravitation, Darwin's theory of evolution, or Einstein's theory of relativity, there is no sense in asking which was the more important for the advancement of science, the speculation or the experiments and observations that led up to it or confirmed it; both speculation and experiments are necessary. No doubt the ability to have the fruitful bright idea is a rarer gift than the ability to carry out the experiments. Much in nature that is obscure to us now may be so because no genius of the order of Newton, Darwin and Einstein has turned up to take the necessary step in speculative thinking. For many years information has been accumulating on telepathy and other phenomena of extra-sensory perception, but no genius has turned up whose speculation can make these things cease to be mysterious and become what we should expect. When he does appear he will do more for our understanding of this field than the mere accumulation of facts in it. But the accumulation of fact is necessary too. Here as elsewhere, speculation is of no use unless it is guided by experiment and observation.

It may also be the case that many of the important practical problems which we cannot yet solve need for their solution new types of thinking even more urgently than they need increased knowledge. It may be that an Einstein of the future will provide us with the way of thinking needed for seeing the solution of such problems as poverty, pollution, over-population, crime, and war.

CHAPTER VII

THE MEANINGS OF WORDS

THERE ARE a number of problems in thinking and communication which are connected with the meanings of words. We may call these *verbal problems*. Perhaps the best way of beginning the study of these problems is to consider what we require words to do for us. We use words, both in thinking and in communication, for such various purposes as describing the reality outside us or our own thoughts and feelings, and for directing our own and other people's actions. In order that we may be able to communicate our thoughts and wishes to other people, it is obviously necessary that they should understand the meanings of the words we use as well as the rules by which we string them together. Their understanding of the meanings of the words we use is sometimes sufficiently assured by the fact that we are using words that are generally understood; sometimes we have to use some special device of explanation, such as a definition, in order to make sure that we shall be understood. But there is also another condition that our words have to fulfil in order that they may be useful for these purposes. They must correspond in some way with the facts we are trying to describe.

For common words, this condition is already fulfilled by the way language has grown up as a means of communicating thoughts and wishes. A device of essential usefulness in the practical use of language is classification; that is, putting groups of objects, actions, etc, into classes and using the same word for all members of the same class. Proper names stand for a single individual: Fido, Rover, Jacko, etc. When we use the one word 'dog' for all of these individuals and any others of their kind, we have formed a class and used a word as the name of that class.

There is no doubt that the word 'dog' is a useful tool of thought. It stands for a class of animals clearly distinguished from other classes of animals. It is a word about whose use there is common agreement, so we are not tempted to use it sometimes with one meaning and sometimes with another. No one will doubt what we mean by it, so we do not have to use some method of defining it in order to make clear to other people what we mean by it.

When we start using words like 'democracy', 'religion', 'freedom', 'goodness', etc, we do not have any of these advantages. They stand for classes not easily separable from other classes. They are not words with an invariable meaning, and we are in great danger of using them with varying meanings. There is no general agreement as to their meaning, so we must define their meaning if we are to be sure of making ourselves understood. In a sense we may say that we want to make our way of using them as much like our way of using such a word as 'dog' as we can. We want different class words to stand for real differences in the world outside that we are describing. In more abstract terms, we may express this by saying that we want the structure of our language to correspond with the structure of the world of fact that we use it to describe. Then our words are useful tools of thought. But if there are differences in the world of fact which have no corresponding differences in our language, or if there are differences in our language which do not correspond to differences in the world of fact, then our use of language is unskilful and is liable to lead us into muddled thinking.

One of the dangers which the careful thinker wants to be able to save himself from is that of using words with indefinite or changing meanings. The most obvious piece of crooked thinking which results from an absence of clear meanings is that in which a word is used in different senses in different parts of the same argument. A popular writer on 'crowd-psychology', for example, began by pointing out the cruelty, irresponsibility, and lack of intelligence of a crowd (that is, of an actual gathering in street or market-place of people with a common interest). He then pointed out that cruelty, irresponsibility, and lack of intelligence are necessary faults of democratic government, because democracy is government by the crowd. Here, however, he has obviously changed the meaning of the word 'crowd', using it first in its literal sense for a group of people in the same place engaged in some common activity, and secondly in a highly metaphorical sense for the voters in a democratic community.

Similarly, in popular discussion of industrial relationships, the terms 'labour' and 'capital' are used both with their strict economic meaning of work and accumulated wealth, and also as meaning 'labourer' and 'capitalist' (which is, for example, the meaning implied in the common conclusion that 'capital and labour are complementary to one another'). The meanings of the terms may shift from one to the other of these in the course of a single argument so that the words are used in one sense in the premisses and in the other in the conclusion.

Just as we have no guarantee of the truth of a conclusion from an argument of sound logical form with doubtful premisses, so also we have no guarantee of the truth of a conclusion from an argument of sound logical form if the terms contained in the argument change their meaning during the course of the argument. Thus the above argument against democratic government might be put into the form:

All crowds are cruel, irresponsible, and unintelligent,
Democracy is government by the crowd,

Therefore, democracy is government by that which is cruel, irresponsible, and unintelligent.

This is clearly an argument in logically correct form, but, even if we were prepared to grant the truth of the somewhat dubious first premiss, the conclusion would not follow, since the word 'crowd' is used with a different meaning in the first and the second premiss.

We must, therefore, distinguish as a type of crooked thinking the use of terms with different meanings in different parts of an argument. We can deal with this by asking a person who is guilty of this to define the terms he uses, and seeing whether the definition he gives for the term at one point in his argument fits the use of the term in other parts of his argument. If we meet such an argument in our reading we may substitute some other form of words for the doubtful term in one place where it is used, and see whether that same form of words will do in the other place. For example, in the passage quoted we find from the examples given of cruelty, irresponsibility, and unintelligence, that the writer here means by 'crowd' a group of people in the same place engaged in some common activity. But this meaning will clearly not do the second time the word 'crowd' is used, since democracy is not government by a group of people in the same place engaged in some common activity. It is clear, therefore, that the argument has been vitiated by a change of meaning in the word 'crowd'.

One of the situations in which there is most danger of our thought going wrong through changing meanings of words is when we are using such national names as Britain, America, Germany, Russia, etc. Muddles in thought matter most when they have serious practical consequences, and few muddles have more serious consequences than the loose use of such national names. Militarism, international misunderstanding, and condonation of cruelty can all result from failure to be clear as to when we are using national names with different meanings.

Let us consider, for example, a speech which might have been given by a patriotic but not very clear-thinking orator on our own side during the 1939 war: 'Germany is the great menace to world peace. She invaded Belgium in 1914 although she had pledged herself by treaty to respect Belgium's neutrality. Although she robbed France of £200,000,000 after the war of 1870, she whined to the Allies about the hardships she would suffer from their reparations demands in 1919, which were her just punishment for her guilt in starting the 1914 war. Do not let Germany's pleas for mercy after her defeat in this war deceive you. Nothing but the annihilation of Germany can secure the future peace of the world.'

The word 'Germany' or a pronoun standing for it occurs twelve times in this passage. The passage can only be a reasonable argument if the word 'Germany' is used to point to the same thing every time it occurs. But does it?

It is by no means clear what 'Germany' stands for in the first sentence. Certainly it does not, either here or anywhere else in the passage, stand for the area of ground which is marked as 'Germany' on a map, for an area of ground cannot menace peace or invade another area of ground, or make and break a pledge, etc. It may stand either for all or for some of the inhabitants of that area of ground or for the more abstract idea of that unity which makes them a separate nation. The practical implications of the sentence do, of course, very considerably depend on which meaning 'Germany' is here meant to have.

The second sentence is easier. The first 'she' (referring, of course, to 'Germany') stands for that part of the German inhabitants who formed the Germany army in 1914, but the second 'she' stands for something quite different. The pledge to respect the neutrality of Belgium was given in 1839, before most of the German inhabitants of 1914 were born. And it was not made by all or any great number of the German inhabitants of that time. It was made by the small ruling group of the very undemocratic state of Prussia, who pledged themselves and all later Governments to respect the neutrality of Belgium. It is true that the rulers of Germany in 1914 were still bound by that agreement, but the form of the sentence implies that the invaders of 1914 and the givers of the pledge were the same, and this erroneous implication is the result of using the word 'Germany' in two senses in the single sentence.

In the next sentence, the first 'she' refers to the rulers in 1871 of the newly founded German Empire, the second 'she' to German newspapers and other forms of publicity in 1919. The 'her' of 'her just punishment' refers to the whole German people (men, women, and children), since all suffered from the impoverishment which was the first result of the reparations demanded by the Treaty of Versailles, whereas the 'her' of 'her guilt' can only refer to those who were guilty of starting the war, who can only be those who were rulers in 1914 or who had sufficient political influence at that time to affect war policy. Plainly we have again the same word used for two groups with some overlap of membership, but many of the second group must have been dead by 1919, and many of the first group were either not born or not grown up in 1914. The suggestion that punishment and guilt are asserted of the same group is the result of using the one word 'Germany' for both groups.

The 'Germany' of the last sentence is presumably the national unit. An area of ground cannot be annihilated, and the most ardent war propagandist does not really want to annihilate all the inhabitants of the enemy country. Germany could clearly be destroyed as a national unit without destroying any of its inhabitants by splitting it up into a number of smaller states or by absorbing it into some other country. The only effect of using the same word 'Germany' in this new sense is to make it sound as if the remedy proposed were more drastic than it really is, as if the speaker were proposing to annihilate the inhabitants of Germany.

It is obvious that if the speaker had wanted to make his meaning perfectly clear he would have had to substitute, for the word 'Germany' each time he used it, some form of words which indicated exactly what he meant each time. Then his speech would run something like this: 'Germany is the great menace to world peace. The German army invaded Belgium in 1914, although the ruling group in Germany at that time inherited the obligation to respect Belgium's neutrality which was entered into by the rulers of Prussia in 1839. Although the rulers of the newly founded German Empire robbed France of £200,000,000 after the war of 1870, the German newspapers and publicists in 1919 whined to the Allies about the hardships that the inhabitants of Germany would suffer from the reparation demands which were the just punishment of the German inhabitants of 1919 for having had in 1914 a Government which was guilty of starting the war. Do not let the pleas of the German publicists for mercy to the German people after the defeat of the German armies in this war deceive you. Nothing but bringing to an end the national autonomy of Germany can secure the future peace of the world.'

The speech still has defects from the point of view of straight thinking (such as the use of such emotional words as *robbed* and *whined*), but in its new form it has the merit of saying exactly what it means without confusion by shifting meanings. For that very reason, it has lost most of its value as propaganda.

One could, of course, equally well illustrate this kind of muddle by constructing an imaginary speech on the other side: 'Germany, the home of poets and musicians, is now in mortal danger. She is fighting for her existence against a ring of enemies who envy her greatness ... etc.' This, too, is non-sense because 'Germany' has not the same meaning throughout. The first 'Germany' obviously refers to the land area marked as Germany on a map, since this alone can be said to be a home of poets and musicians. But the land area itself cannot fight; the 'she' in the next sentence refers to that part of the adult population that is in the fighting forces or otherwise actively engaged in the war effort. But the 'her' of 'her existence' cannot have either of these meanings. Neither the land area nor the population would cease to exist as a result of defeat in warfare. Here we have the more abstract meaning of the national entity called 'Germany'; that might come to an end if the nation were split up into smaller units or absorbed by some other nation, although its former population as well as its former land area went on existing as parts of the new national units. Obviously there is not much coherence left in this speech when we have critically examined what is meant by 'Germany' each time the word is used.

The speeches given above belong, of course, to past history and are about a quarrel which is no longer of living interest. But the problem itself is not dead. We can still think and talk about our own country or about the most hated national group of the moment with the same danger of muddle through not realising exactly what the national name stands for whenever it occurs. Whenever we see or use such phrases as 'X did so-and-so', 'the greatness of X', or 'the interests of X', we can perform for ourselves the exercise of finding out in what sense X (the name of any national group) is used in each case. Particularly we should be clear when X stands for the whole group of inhabitants, Dick, Karl, or Vladimir, with their wives and children, and when it does not. The 'interests of X' may or may not refer to the interests of Dick, Karl or Vladimir, with their wives and children. Even so, these interests may be of such importance that men should be ready to sacrifice their lives for them, but they may not. It is better that we should know what 'X' refers to before we prepare to sacrifice our lives for its interests. It may be a small group of men in ruling positions or exerting influence by their wealth, with whose interests we should not feel ourselves much concerned.

The habit of using words with two or more meanings not clearly distinguished may lead us into much erroneous thinking. A much worse form of the same disease is that of using a word with no clear meaning but with only a general tendency in some direction. Then we are guilty of vagueness, which is a fault that makes accurate thought and reasonable discussion impossible.

In order to be vague it is not necessary that a statement should also be obscure. It often is, and more or less deliberate obscurity is often a cloak for vagueness. But the simplest statement or thought may be vague if it does not embody a clear meaning in the mind of the person making it. This is particularly liable to happen with abstract words. Such words, for example, as 'principle', 'wealth', 'spiritual', have meanings which can never be carried by a mental image of an outside object or action or of a relation between outside objects or actions. Their proper meaning is a kind of summary or abstraction of many different outside things.

We all of us hear many such words which at the beginning carry no meaning for us at all, and we are quite likely to take them over into our vocabulary before they have a clear meaning. To obtain clear meanings for any but the common names of outside things requires a certain amount of mental effort, and idleness leads us to be content with taking many words into our speech and thought without making this mental effort.

Let us first consider how to get rid of vagueness from our own minds before we consider how we can combat our opponent's vagueness in argument. We can begin by looking up definitions. Habitual recourse to the dictionary whenever we meet with a new word before taking it into our vocabulary is a useful rule which helps against the development of words without definite meanings in our vocabularies.

While the use of dictionary definition should save us from using words with shifting and variable meanings, it does not do everything that is necessary to make them a serviceable part of our mental equipment for straight thinking. Let us suppose, for example, that we have met with a technical term that is new to us. We wish to understand it when we read it, and also to be able to use it in our own talking and writing. We look the word up in a standard dictionary or in a technical dictionary of psychological, philosophical or economic terms. If the dictionary is a good one, we shall now have a clear and unambiguous account of how the word is used, either in general speech from the standard dictionary or in one of the language systems of the sciences if we have consulted a technical dictionary. We shall discover from the dictionary how to describe the use of the new term and we shall also know from the dictionary definition that a number of ways of using it that we might previously have been tempted to adopt are erroneous.

Knowing how to describe the use of a word is not, however, enough to ensure that we shall either understand its use or be ourselves able to use it in the proper way. The situation is rather as if we had read an accurate description of a deep-sea fish, but found this description insufficient to enable us to draw the fish or even to recognise it if we saw it.

We may, for example, meet the psychoanalytic term 'complex' and look it up in a psychological dictionary and find some such definition as the following: 'COMPLEX: an unconscious or partly unconscious system of ideas linked together to form a chain in some potential behaviour reaction.' This is not perhaps a very good definition but it is sufficient to give an idea of the sort of thing the word 'complex' stands for. It is obviously not sufficient to enable the person who reads it to use the word in the intended manner. He would, at least, want some illustrations of what systems of ideas the word would be applied to. He would need to know that an example of a complex might be a long-forgotten fright experienced in childhood from an oncoming train which produced in later life a persistent terror of going more than a few hundred yards from home, or a forgotten childish resentment against one's father producing a later hatred of kings, judges, policemen, and all in authority. After having heard these illustrations, he may be able to say: 'Now I begin to see what you mean by "complex"'. These two examples of complexes are not likely in themselves to make the meaning of the word sufficiently definite to make it a serviceable part of his mental equipment. They, together with the definition, may act as guides to the experience of studying his own and other people's mental life and what he reads in psychoanalytic literature until he has a definite understanding and use of the word. So by the combined effect of definition, illustration and experience, he has gained a knowledge of the meaning of the word 'complex' which will save him both from the danger of using it vaguely and also from the danger of using it without reference to anything real in the world around him.

The giving of illustrations is a useful device for keeping one's thinking in close contact with earth. It is a sound plan, in the course of reading, talking, or thinking, to challenge ourselves to give particular examples as illustrations of general statements. Otherwise the abstract terms we use may be so devoid of meaning to us that our thought has lost touch with reality.

We read, for example, in a book on psychology: 'The social value of instinct transformation lies in the fact that it can provide a socially harmless outlet for otherwise objectionable behaviour tendencies.' We pause and think, 'It is a good thing for Tommy to play football, because he is then less likely to make a nuisance of himself by fighting other boys or by throwing stones at street lamps.' That is one example of what the passage means, so we can be sure that we are not altogether failing to follow the author's meaning. We need not for the moment also stop to think of all the other things it means: the value of writing poetry to Shelley, of tournaments to King Arthur's knights, of keeping cats to those who are lonely, and a great deal more.

We read on, and again come to a passage where we are led to pause to be certain that we have understood: 'Deprivation of the nutritive instinct is destructive of the higher cultural interests.' We reflect that a man who hasn't enough to eat does not bother about poetry or pictures.

We turn to another book and are held up by the passage: 'Pain and pleasant sensation gives us the instinct mentality, the content of feeling functions dynamically, as the entity of instinct action.' We try to think of a particular thing that this could mean. The first four words present no difficulty, but afterwards we are baffled. We do not understand it, and can make no use of it in our thought. We go back to earlier explanations of the technical terms used; we may even read the whole of the book again in the hope that it will become clear on a second or third reading. If still no particular thing seems to us to illustrate the passage we must reluctantly conclude that we do not understand it. This may be the author's fault or our own.

We must not, of course, make the mistake of supposing that a single simple illustration exhausts the meaning of an abstract passage. The abstract terminology is a shorthand way of expressing a large collection of particular facts. Success in abstract thinking means that we really can think of the whole class in its common features and not only of the particular members of it which we may have chosen for illustration. Until we can do this we have not advanced to the level of abstract thought. Ability to think in abstract terms is one of the skills we have to acquire. We begin to learn it in school and we should go on learning it for the rest of our lives.

CHAPTER VIII

DEFINITION AND SOME OF ITS DIFFICULTIES

IF OUR thought is to be clear and we are to succeed in communicating it to other people, we must have some method of fixing the meanings of the words we use. When we use a word whose meaning is not certain we may well be asked to define it. There is a useful traditional device for doing this by indicating the class to which whatever is indicated by the term belongs, and also the particular property which distinguishes it from all other members of the same class. Thus we may define a whale as a 'marine animal that spouts'. 'Marine animal' in this definition indicates the general class to which the whale belongs, and 'spouts' indicates the particular property that distinguishes whales from such other marine animals as fishes, seals, jelly-fish, lobsters, etc. In the same way, we can define an even number as a finite integer divisible by two, or a democracy as a system of government in which the people themselves rule.

There are other ways, of course, of indicating the meanings of words. We may, for example, find it hard to make a suitable definition of the word 'animal', so we say that an animal is such a thing as a rabbit, dog, fish, etc. Similarly we may say that a religion is such a system as Christianity, Islam, Judaism, Christian Science, etc. This way of indicating the meaning of a term by enumerating examples of what it includes is obviously of limited usefulness. If we indicated our use of the word 'animal' as above, our hearers might, for example, be doubtful whether a sea-anemone or a slug was to be included in the class of animals. It is, however, a useful way of supplementing a definition if the definition itself is definite without being easily understandable. If, for example, we explain what we mean by 'religion' by saying: 'A religion is a system of beliefs and practices connected with a spiritual world, such as Christianity, Islam, Judaism, Christian Science, and so on', we may succeed in making our meaning more clear than it would be if we had given the definition alone.

Failure of an attempt at definition to serve its purpose may result from giving as distinguishing mark one which either does not belong to all the things the definition is intended to include, or does belong to some members of the same general class which the definition is intended to exclude. Thinking, for example, of the most obvious difference between a rabbit and a cabbage, we might be tempted to define an animal as a living organism which is able to move about. This would combine both faults mentioned above, since some animals (e.g., some shell-fish such as the oyster) are not able to move about for the whole or for part of their lives, while some vegetables (such as the fresh-water alga *Volvox*) do swim about. Of course, any-one who used the above definition might claim to be defining 'animal' in a new and original way to include *Volvox* and exclude oysters, but he would have failed to produce a definition which defined the ordinary use of the word 'animal'.

More commonly an attempt at definition fails by not indicating correctly the general class to which the thing defined belongs. One meets for example, in psychological writings such definitions as: 'Intelligence is a state of mind characterized by the ability to learn and to solve problems'. The second part of the definition is all right, but the word 'intelligence' is not used for a state of mind; and the person who defines 'intelligence' like this does not in his actual use of the word make it stand for a state of mind. Such conditions as despair, concentration, alertness, and hope can be called 'states of mind'. 'Intelligence' is used for a quality of mind, not for a state. If the word 'quality' replaced the word 'state' in the above definition it would indicate very well the current use of the word 'intelligence' in the language system of psychology. This may not, of course, be identical with the use of the word in everyday speech. There its meaning is likely to be found to be wider and less definite.

Indication of the use of class names by the method of definition is easy when things fall easily into classes. It becomes more difficult when one is dealing with things that do not fall easily into classes. Then many pitfalls lie in the path of the careless thinker. There is a venerable law of logic called the 'law of excluded middle' which states that A is either B or not B. Thus a piece of paper is either white or not white. There is a sense in which this is obviously true, yet the kind of thinking embodied in this law may be dangerous and misleading when applied to a certain common range of facts.

Let us consider the case of white paper. The whiteness of paper depends on the amount of light that it reflects to our eyes. We should call the paper on which this book is printed 'white' because it reflects a great deal of light and absorbs very little. Yet it does not reflect all. If we coated it with certain chemical substances it would reflect more, but still it would not reflect all the light falling on it. If we coated it very lightly with something that made it reflect less light, we might still call it white. As we increased the depth of the coating, however, we should soon reduce the brightness of the surface so much that we should be compelled to call it a light grey, afterwards a dark grey, and finally black. The fact that we called it black, however, would not mean that the surface reflected no light. If we coated it with lamp-black it would reflect still less light, and would, therefore, be even blacker, but it would still be reflecting some of the light that fell on it.

It seems, then, that white, grey, and black papers do not fall into naturally separable classes. The trouble lies in the fact that whiteness is a property which papers can have in any quantity, that no paper is 100 per cent white and that there is no real dividing line between papers that have enough of this property to be called white and those that have not. We want, however, to use the words 'white', 'grey', and 'black' because they stand for real and important differences, and if we are to use them exactly, we must adopt some such device as definition for making their meanings clear.

For most practical purposes we do not have to be exact in our use of these terms, and it does not matter very much that one person will call a paper 'light grey' when another calls it 'dirty white', but there might be purposes for which it was necessary to leave no doubt of our use of these terms – for example, if the paper is required for house decoration. We should then be driven to make arbitrary dividing lines for our classification, defining a white paper, for example, as one that reflected at least 80 per cent of the light falling on it, and a black paper as one that reflected not more than 6 per cent of the light falling on it, while a grey paper was defined as one that lay anywhere between those limits.

Although what we have done in making these definitions is quite proper and may be useful, yet we have introduced a certain danger of crooked thinking, for we have used three words – 'white', 'grey', and 'black' – as if they stood for distinct classes, whereas there is continuous variation by imperceptible steps from the purest white to the deepest black. Such a way of thinking can lead our thought into muddles, since it may lead us to overlook the fact that we may have two white papers (reflecting, let us say, 81 per cent and 95 per cent) and a grey paper (reflecting 79 per cent) such that the difference between the grey and one of the whites is far less than the difference between the two whites. In other words, it may lead us to think that there are sharper distinctions than there really are.

We could, of course, deal with the facts in another way which avoided this danger. We can consider whiteness as a property arranged along a line which has at one end the property of reflecting 100 per cent of light (pure whiteness) and, at the other end, the property of reflecting 0 per cent light (pure blackness). Between these two extremes we can construct a scale showing all the intermediate percentages of light that can be reflected. Every piece of white, grey, or black paper can be assigned to some position on this scale. We can then say that such a piece of paper reflects 95 per cent of the light falling on it, another reflects 85 per cent, another 65 per cent, another 50 per cent, and another 10 per cent. We have by this method indicated the facts much more precisely than we could by calling the first two papers white, the next two grey, and the last black. At the same time, we shall retain 'white,' 'grey', and 'black' as practically convenient words, while realizing clearly that they do not stand for sharply distinguishable classes of properties.

Any muddles in thought that result from ignoring this property of continuous variation in whiteness, greyness, and blackness are, of course, unimportant. But precisely similar muddles occur in other fields of thought which are important. All over human life we find properties which show continuous variation, and (just as in the case of white and black) we find this property obscured by the use of words implying sharp distinctions. 'Sane' and 'insane'; 'good' and 'bad'; 'intelligent' and 'unintelligent'; 'proletarian' and 'capitalist', are pairs of opposites which show this property of continuous variation. Our use of the two sharply contrasted terms 'sane' of ourselves and our neighbours, and 'insane' of the unfortunate persons confined in mental hospitals, leads us to forget the continuity between them. The essential difference between the sane and insane is, however, simply the degree to which they are able to adapt themselves to their environments. This power of successful adaptation varies quite continuously from one individual to another; no one has it perfectly and probably no one has quite lost it. We could make a continuous row of people progressively less well adapted, with the sanest of ourselves at one end and the most insane inhabitants of mental hospitals at the other. It is therefore not reasonable to say any such thing as: 'A man must be either sane or insane, and if he is insane he must be incapable of rational thinking.' Any argument beginning in this way is a dangerous piece of crooked thinking which ignores the fact of continuity.

Intelligence has been mentioned as one of the examples of continuous variation being obscured in ordinary thinking. When we use such words as 'idiot', 'imbecile', 'backward', 'normal', 'bright', 'genius', we are inclined to think of people as divided by their inborn gifts into really distinct classes. Measurement of intelligence by intelligence-tests shows that this is not the case. If we take a thousand children and measure their intelligence by testing we shall find that every degree of intelligence from about 30 per cent to 170 per cent of the normal is represented amongst them, that the commonest values are the central ones (about normal), while there are fewer of the extremely high and the extremely low values. There are no natural dividing lines between the different classes 'idiot', 'imbecile', etc; in making these distinctions we are drawing lines where none exist in fact. This is often a practically convenient thing to do, but if it misleads us into thinking that the real difference between 'intellectually deficient' and 'normal' children is as sharp as the difference between the words we use, we have been led into crooked thinking.

The error here lies in the fact that by using separate words to distinguish two extremes showing continuous variation between them, we are making a sharp distinction appear where there is none in fact. A great deal of our thinking has to be revised if we are to recognize the continuity between sanity and insanity, between intelligence and unintelligence, between goodness and badness, between crime and socialized behaviour, between religion and irreligion, and between civilization and uncivilization. The difficulty is recognized in everyday speech as that of knowing 'where to draw the line'. Where no sharp dividing lines exist in fact, the use of sharply different words to distinguish classes of facts which show continuous variation may distort the realities we are talking about.

The way in which the ignoring of continuous variation leads to crooked argumentation may be illustrated as follows. The speaker tries to impose on us a sharp distinction by offering us a dilemma, such as: 'You will admit that a child is either capable of profiting by normal schooling or else is an idiot.' He will then go on to assert that it is nonsense to provide special schools for those who are intellectually retarded without being idiots or to adopt different methods of teaching for normal children of different intellectual capacity. All arguments that begin: 'An X must be either Y or not-Y . . .' – must be treated as unsound if Y is a characteristic that shows continuous variation, and should be dealt with by pointing out that the sharp distinction between Y and not-Y implied by the speaker is not in accordance with the facts.

This is the first kind of crooked thinking into which we may be led when dealing with facts showing continuous variation – that we may make sharp distinctions in speech where none exists in fact. There is another which is the opposite of this: we may deny the reality of differences because there is continuous variation between the different things. We should immediately reject as absurd the contention of someone who claimed that there was no difference between white and black because we can pass from one to the other by a continuous series of small steps, but an exactly parallel argument is often used to deny the reality of differences in matters that are of more practical importance.

A very old example illustrates the kind of error that is involved. One may throw doubt on the reality of the difference between a bearded and a clean-shaven man by a process beginning with the question whether a man with one hair on his chin has a beard. The answer is clearly 'No'. Then one may ask whether with two hairs on his chin a man has a beard. Again the answer must be 'No'. So again with three, four, etc. At no point can our opponent say 'Yes', for if he has answered 'No' for, let us say, twenty-nine hairs, and 'Yes' for thirty, it is easy to pour scorn on the suggestion that the difference between twenty-nine and thirty hairs is the difference between not having and having a beard. Yet by this process of adding one hair at a time we can reach a number of hairs which would undoubtedly make up a beard. The trouble is that the difference between a beard and no beard is like the difference between black and white, a difference between two extremes that have no sharp dividing line between them but a continuous gradation.

In this argument, the fact of continuous variation has been used to undermine the reality of the difference. Because there is no sharp dividing line, it has been suggested that there is no difference. This is clearly a piece of crooked argument which would take in no reasonable person, so long, at any rate, as it was used about beards and not about anything which engaged our emotions more strongly.

A similar error lay at the back of the mind of the man who loaded his camel one straw at a time, hoping that the additional weight of a single straw would never be enough to injure the camel. When at length the camel's back broke, he attributed it to the extra weight of the last straw. He supposed that because there was no sharp line between a moderate load and a severe over-load, there was therefore no difference between them. Again this is a mistake which no reasonable person would make.

We do, however, frequently hear an argument against the distinction between a proletarian and a capitalist which begins: 'When does a man become a capitalist? If a working man has £200 in the bank, is he a capitalist?' This is the argument of the beard. Those who would not be deceived in connection with beards readily swallow the same piece of crooked thinking when it is used in connection with matters on which their emotions are stronger. The truth is, of course, that the difference between those who own capital and those who do not is one of the most important of the social differences between men, although there is continuous variation between those who own nothing and those who own a great deal. It is equally wrong to suppose that there is a sharp dividing line between these classes and to suppose that there is no difference between them. The justification for using the terms 'capitalist' and 'proletarian' in social thinking is the same as the justification for using the words 'white' and 'black', and the use of the words is open to precisely the same dangers of creating sharply distinct classes where none exist in fact. This danger, however, is not to be dealt with by denying the reality of the difference.

The argument of the beard is also sometimes used against the important distinction between neutral and emotionally charged words discussed in the first chapter of the present book. It has been suggested that this distinction cannot be a real one because the words we use may be more or less emotionally charged so that we can draw no sharp line between those that are neutral and those that are emotionally charged. This, of course, is the case, but this is not inconsistent with there being a real and important difference between an almost completely neutral term such as 'not easily influenced' and the highly charged term 'pig-headed'. One may also pass by continuous stages from animal to vegetable forms of life, but there remains an important difference between a rabbit and a lettuce which is indicated by calling one an 'animal' and the other a 'vegetable'.

The argument of the beard is one that has a curious and undeserved intellectual respectability because it is much more used by clever people than by simple ones. It is one of the pitfalls of thought into which one will not fall unless one has a rather ingenious and subtle cast of mind. Amongst the clever, it is a common fallacy which crops up frequently in different contexts. I found an example in a correspondence in a leading newspaper on the subject of corporal punishment. One writer argued that there was really no difference between corporal and other punishments in school because all punishments affect the body to some extent. If a boy is kept in, it is his body that is kept in, and if he is rebuked, the rebuke may have bodily effects such as blushing, etc.

This is again a form of the argument of the beard. 'Corporal punishment' means punishment of the body, such as beating with the hand or some such implement as a cane, strap, etc. It may be a better or worse way of punishing than giving lines, keeping in, or rebuking, but one is merely muddling oneself and making more difficult a rational decision as to the merits of different kinds of punishment by refusing to admit that they really are different kinds of punishment, and that one kind may be preferable to another.

In these regions of thought in which one class of things shows an indefinite series of steps by which it passes to its opposite, it is still necessary to use words with exact indications of their meanings. We may also still use definition as a way of showing what we mean, although it will often be necessary for our definitions to indicate arbitrary dividing lines (such as the 80 per cent reflection of light in our definition of 'white'). Yet the practice of defining one's terms may have dangers, since it tends to create ideas that are too precise to fit the facts they are intended to describe. This may be no help to clear thinking if it marks off sharply in our thought what is not sharply marked off in fact.

The device of badgering one's opponent to define his terms may sometimes be a piece of crooked argumentation, since it may be an invitation to him to provide clear-cut ideas which have little relation to the complexity of the facts under discussion. Sometimes formal definition is refused in order to avoid this danger while some other method is adopted of making one's meaning clear.

There is another misuse of the definition which is perhaps worth mentioning. The purpose of a definition should be to make clear how you are going to use words, not to indicate your attitude towards the thing defined. A typical muddle that results from not making this distinction is that provided by those who think that they prove their breadth of mind by defining, let us say, 'religion' widely as perhaps 'a sense of the Beyond', in contrast with such narrow-minded persons as Mr Thwackum of *The History of Tom Jones*, who when he mentioned 'religion' meant the Christian religion, and not only the Christian religion but the Protestant religion, and not only the Protestant religion but the Church of England.

In reality there is no moral value attached to a wide or a narrow use of a word; neither tolerance nor charity towards those who differ from us in religion depend on our use of the word. It is purely a question of practical convenience. Mr Thwackum's narrow use of the word 'religion' has two inconveniences. First, it uses the word 'religion' for something which is already named 'the Church of England'; there is obviously no point in having two different words to stand for the same thing. Secondly, and more seriously, it leaves us without a name for the class which includes Christianity, Buddhism, Islam, Judaism, ancestor-worship, Voodoo, etc.

If we are not to use the word 'religion' for this class, we must find some other word for it. So all Mr Thwackum has done is to take a word from serving a useful purpose and put it where it serves no purpose. What, of course, he was trying to say was that he thought the religion of the Church of England was the only true religion, but that can obviously be best said without changing the meaning of the word 'religion'.

There are other objections from the point of view of convenience to defining 'religion' as 'a sense of the Beyond'. The definition is so vague that it does not fulfil the primary purpose of a definition, that of making clear to what it is meant to be applied. Anyone who has looked at the stars and realized that there must be many more stars too faint to see may be said to have a sense of the Beyond. So also may anyone who has counted through as many numbers as he can and realizes that there are others that his counting can never reach. It does not seem likely that such reflections are meant to be included in the word 'religion' when this is defined as a sense of the Beyond, but the definition might be taken to include them. There is also the same objection to this definition as was made to Mr Thwackum's definition that if we are to use the word 'religion' in this way, we are left without a name for the class that includes Christianity, Buddhism, Islam, etc. But we want a name for this class if we are ever to think or talk about it.

Definition is a process intended to make our thought clear and our speech understandable to others. The use of definition as a means of indicating opinions or valuations defeats its proper aim.

CHAPTER IX

TRICKS OF SUGGESTION

SOME OF the methods used by the orator to create agreement with what he has to say are similar to devices used to produce the condition of trance known as the 'hypnotic state', in which the hypnotizer fixes his patient with a steady gaze and in a firm, confident manner tells him that he is falling asleep. We sometimes read that powerfully persuasive orators 'hypnotize their audiences' into believing what is required of them. That, of course, can never be literally true. The hypnotic trance is a condition startlingly different from the alert state of everyday life, and an audience that was literally hypnotized would attract as much attention as one that was dead drunk. Such an expression must only be understood as the same kind of inexact metaphor as when we speak of another audience being 'intoxicated with enthusiasm'. So we shall prefer the more exact technical, psychological term and call these oratorical devices 'tricks of suggestion'.

The psychological fact of suggestion is the fact that if statements are made again and again in a confident manner, without argument or proof, then their hearers will tend to believe them quite independently of their soundness and of the presence or absence of evidence for their truth. More particularly will his hearers tend to accept the suggestions of a speaker if he has what we may call 'prestige' – the acknowledged dignity of authority possessed by Cabinet Ministers, bishops, athletes, astronauts, authors, and other famous men.

An orator using the method of suggestion relies, then, on

three things: (1) repeated affirmation, (2) a confident, insistent method of speaking, and (3) prestige.

First, let us be clear as to what we mean by 'repeated affirmation'. We may contrast two ways of trying to make somebody else agree with us. One is to put forward the reasons we have for our belief. If we do this, we must be prepared also to consider his reasons for disagreeing with us and to weigh against each other the worth of his reasons and of our own. Obviously this is a laborious method, and one that is not likely to lead to a feeling of absolute certainty on the matter in dispute. It has the advantage that it is the one method which may help both disputants to some sight, however dim, of the truth.

Such an advantage will not weigh heavily in favour of this method in the minds of those who wish for quick results – who prefer that people should act blindly and enthusiastically under their guidance rather than that they should decide calmly and wisely. For these, another method is open – that of simply saying the thing which is to be believed over and over again. This is 'repeated affirmation'.

No one could have told from first principles that mere repetition of a statement would make the hearers tend to believe that statement. That is a fact which had to be discovered – the fact that may be described by the phrase 'human suggestibility'. It has been known as a matter of practice by those wishing to influence opinion even when they have never heard the words 'suggestion' and 'suggestibility'. In the old days, when a candidate for Parliament could spend as much as he liked on election propaganda, he would often placard the walls of his town with innumerable notices which simply said VOTE FOR SIMPKINS or VOTE FOR ROBERTS. If these notices had the intended effect of increasing the tendency of electors to vote for the named candidate, they did so by the use of suggestion by repeated affirmation. They did not give any reason for supposing that the named candidate would be a better member of parliament than his rival. The notices relied on suggestion alone.

The suggestion would act more powerfully if it were made also by means of speech and not merely in print, so Simpkins himself toured his constituency and made speeches in which he said: 'I shall win', and 'Sane and stable government can only be ensured to the country by the victory of the X party'. His speech would be monotonous if he merely said these things over and over again in the same words, so he said them over and over again in different words. 'The country will be led to prosperity by our honoured and trusted leader, John Smith', 'The British people will never support the unprincipled Y party or the wild experimentation of the Z party', 'Our country needs (and will now have) a period of government by men of sound principle'. These phrases are quite differently worded, but they contain nothing but the two very simple ideas with which we started – 'I shall win' and 'Sane and stable government can only be ensured to the country by the victory of the X party'.

The orator is using the method of repetition although he repeats himself in different words partly to avoid monotony and partly to conceal the method actually used. A speech of this kind is like a piece of music made up of one or two short tunes which occur again and again with slight variations. I once analyzed part of a sermon constructed on this principle, and found that the preacher had in quite different forms repeated a single idea thirty-one times in the course of thirteen sentences.

A more recent example is a public speech by a British statesman who was reported to have said: 'Your government, Mr Chairman, will not fail; we will succeed. The people will not lose; the people will win. The nation will not be dragged down. The nation will emerge triumphant.'

This is using the same technique as the preacher, that of repetition with variation. There are three variations of the theme 'We shall succeed', each stated once negatively and once positively. It is true that this only gives six repetitions in all, but this is only an extract from the speech; there may have been a larger number of repetitions in the whole speech.

No doubt this was effective if it was well delivered; its hearers were probably left with the conviction that the government was going to succeed. It has, however, the weakness of any purely irrational method of appeal, that the same basic material might be delivered equally effectively in the opposite sense by a speaker of the other side:' The Conservative government, Mr Chairman, will not succeed; it will fail. The people will not win; the people will lose. The nation will not emerge triumphant; the nation will be dragged down.'

If this were equally forcibly delivered by a speaker of equal standing, this would be likely to be as persuasive as in the first form. Neither would have much effect if it were delivered to an audience sufficiently aware of the devices of crooked communication to recognize either speech as an exercise in repeated affirmation.

But the speaker does not rely merely on repetition. There are manners of repetition more successful than others. A half-hearted, hesitating kind of delivery has little suggestive effect. So the speaker develops the opposite manner of brazen confidence. Whatever doubts and hesitations and timidities he may feel are not allowed to appear in his manner. He thrusts out his chest, lifts up his head, and talks in a steady, loud voice. This is his confident manner, which is the second aid to success in suggestion. An inner feeling of certainty that one is right may be a valuable help in producing the manner, but is not essential to it. A practised speaker who has learned the trick of the confident manner can put it on like a mask. A political candidate will find it a greater help to his success than any amount of expert knowledge on the work of government which he is proposing to undertake.

He must be on his guard, however, against hostile hecklers who may know very well how to destroy his confident manner. If they can interject a question which makes the audience laugh at the candidate, or which makes him lose his temper even a little, the confident manner is difficult to maintain. Some practised speakers under hostile interruption make plaintive appeals to the sympathy of their audience. These may be successful, but the full force of the confident manner cannot be brought into use again.

The candidate will also rely on his prestige. As external aids to this he will probably dress himself in a formal manner. Since a convention of modesty prevents him from telling us himself what a great man he is, he will have an election agent who will increase the candidate's prestige by praise of him before he comes in. Most powerfully of all, however, will the effect of prestige work when the candidate gets a peer of the realm or a Cabinet Minister to speak for him. People are more suggestible to those in high places than to anyone else. That the peer's prestige may be entirely due to an inherited title and not at all to any personal qualities of his own will not prevent his suggestions from having more prestige effect than those of the Cabinet Minister. The workings of such automatic operations of our mind as suggestibility are not altogether reasonable.

If a speaker wants to put something across to an audience by the use of suggestion, he is fortunate if his title, occupation, or worldly situation gives him prestige. If he has none of these sources of prestige, he must either depend on his own gifts as an orator or else invent sources of prestige. Many years ago I saw a man in an English market-place who was trying to sell patent medicines. He was introduced as professor of physiology at a well-known Northern university and a great authority on physical training. He mounted a tub and began by telling us that he did not generally speak from a tub but from his own Rolls-Royce. In fact, he was clearly not a professor of physiology, and there was no reason for supposing that he was the owner of a Rolls-Royce, which would have implied that he was a wealthy and successful man. These were fictions designed to increase his prestige. Professors have a certain amount of prestige, and wealthy men have perhaps more.

I did not wait to see how much medicine he succeeded in selling; probably not much. His technique of prestige magnification was not good. His manner lacked self-confidence and he needed a shave. A real shave would have done more towards bolstering up his prestige than his imaginary Rolls-Royce.

There are other dishonest ways of bolstering up one's prestige. For example, the trick of using obscure technical jargon in a discussion is often a device for acquiring undeserved prestige. The squire in *The Vicar of Wakefield* confuted his unsophisticated opponent by asking: 'Whether do you judge the analytical investigation of the first part of my enthymem deficient secundum quoad, or quoad minus?'

The device of using a technical jargon (or something which sounds like a technical jargon) for the purpose of mystifying one's hearers is not often employed as blatantly as in the passage quoted above. We do, however, often hear people talking in an unnecessarily obscure way. This may sometimes be due to the speaker's incompetence in the use of words or to idleness, which leads him not to take the trouble to put simply what he wants to say. It is also, no doubt, sometimes used deliberately by those who have discovered that many people are more easily impressed by what they cannot understand.

In trying to protect ourselves against such an abuse of language, we must bear in mind that our failure to understand does not necessarily imply that our opponent is trying to mystify us. He may be making a perfectly proper use of the technical language of whatever branch of knowledge he is talking about. The use of a technical language not understandable to anyone who has not troubled to master it is a necessity in any branch of learning. It is a kind of intellectual shorthand which enables one to say in a sentence what could otherwise only be explained in many pages. When we meet obscurity in verbal discussion, the best reply is to ask one's opponent to explain more simply what he means. If he cannot explain himself in simple language, even though he has the opportunity of doing so at great length, we may reasonably suspect him of not understanding what he means himself. It does not necessarily follow that he is using technical terms for prestige effect; it may be only that he has not the necessary skill in the use of language to express himself simply. In either case we shall not allow ourselves to be impressed by his obscurity as if this were a sign of his superior understanding.

Obscurity in reading matter is more difficult to deal with, since we cannot ask the author what he means. But in writing, as in speech, the mere fact that we do not understand is not in itself proof that the author is trying to impress us by deliberate obscurity. He may be talking good sense in a language we do not understand. Every science has its technical vocabulary, and it is no more reasonable to expect to be able to understand a book on psychology, physics, or mathematics without first learning the technical languages of those sciences than it is to expect to be able to read a book written in Dutch if we have not first learnt Dutch.

Yet the existence of technical languages gives an opportunity to those who want to use them for prestige effect, and a great deal of the obscurity of books on most subjects is not due to the use of a technical language because this is the most economical way of communicating what their authors have to say. Books are often obscure because those who write them do not themselves think clearly or because they want the prestige rewards of obscurity. On the other hand an author may be obscure because he is struggling against a difficulty in communication which he can only overcome by the creation of a language of his own. The great philosopher Kant was obscure, and many of his contemporaries judged that, therefore, he was vague and meaningless. They were wrong. But on the whole it is more probable that what is judged to be mere vagueness and emptiness of thought by those who have been trained in overcoming the legitimate obscurities of technical language is really so. The number of books that are hopelessly vague and relatively empty of meaning is large; much larger than a charitable reader would wish to suppose.

There is no sure way of distinguishing them. There are certain writers whose books any student of the subject knows are of real value, whose obscurities must be overcome by effort on the part of the reader. The student knows also the names of a much larger number of others whose obscurities are not likely to be worth penetrating. None of us can hope to have this knowledge except in a very small field of learning. Outside that field we must rely on the judgement of others or else be prepared to waste a great deal of our own time.

Many of the tricks of dishonest argument which have been described earlier can be most easily carried through with a backing of prestige. A diversion (pp 44 ff), for example, can most easily be forced or a fallacy escape notice when a person of greater prestige is arguing against someone else with much less (let us say a professor against a student or a Member of Parliament against one of his constituents). Indeed, the harmless protective device suggested against obscure language – that of confessing failure to understand and asking for explanation – may become a deadly weapon of dishonest argument in the hands of a man relying on his prestige. Let us suppose, for example, that a professor is asked an awkward question by one of his students and that he prefers a cheap victory to an honest discussion. He may say: 'I am afraid, Mr Smith, that I cannot understand what you mean. You are too subtle for me.' It is clear that the impression left on the mind of an audience will be that the student must have been talking nonsense, for they cannot suppose that otherwise the professor would have been unable to understand him.

Perhaps the best way to counter this trick is one suggested by Schopenhauer. Like a ju-jitsu wrestler, instead of opposing the weight of his antagonist the student may give way to it, in order thus to overthrow him. He may say, for example: 'It must be my fault that you don't understand me. I'll try to put it in another way.' He can then explain what he means so fully and clearly that the simplest onlooker must understand that he has made his point.

Other controversial devices depending on suggestion are those in which the answer is in some way dictated by the question. Most simply this happens when the question suggests its own answer, as: 'Surely you accept the principles of the Reformation?' or 'You accept the principles of the Reformation, don't you?' If the person questioned is showing himself resistant to suggestion, this method can be reversed and a question asked which implies the opposite answer to that required; the questioner frames his question so as to appear to be trying to force the answer 'No', when he really wants his opponent to answer 'Yes'.

A variant of the same method is the well-known trick of asking a question so framed that any direct answer to it will imply an admission damaging to your case. 'Will agriculture benefit by the increased prices which will follow the imposition of taxes on imported food?' Clearly, either of the answers 'Yes' or 'No' implies the admission that such taxes would raise food prices, which the person disputing may not be willing to admit. The same end can be attained by asking many different things as a complicated question demanding a single answer, as, for example, 'Do you admit that the enemy have murdered their prisoners, bombed defenceless towns, fired on the Red Cross, and sunk hospital ships? Yes or no.' Plainly the person questioned might wish to answer 'Yes' to some of these questions, 'No' to others, and to make some qualifications to his answers to others. Either of the answers invited will land him in many admissions he does not want to make.

It is obvious that the first trick must be met by refusing to be influenced by the suggestion, and the second and third by dividing up the question and answering different parts separately. So obvious is this that one might wonder why such tricks are ever successful. It is because the tricks are used with an overbearing technique of suggestion. Without that they would have no force, and with it the correct reply may be almost impossibly difficult.

The remedy would seem to be that we should liberate ourselves, so far as we can, from the influence of suggestion. This is partly a matter of self-education. The more we know about the psychological nature of suggestion, the less will be its power over us in the ordinary situations of everyday life. Certainly we may not be able to escape its effects in all circumstances even when we have a good understanding of its nature. We may, for example, be in the situation of being questioned by someone who not only has an authoritative manner but also has real authority over us (he may be able, for example, to deprive us of employment or to send us to prison). Any use he makes of the techniques of prestige suggestion will be made more effective by the favourable situation which he is in. We may, however, succeed in reducing their effect by ourselves using as much of the confident manner as we judge to be safe. Some people have reported the successful use of mental devices to reduce the questioner's prestige, such as that of picturing to oneself what he would look like with nothing on.

There are, however, also situations in which the odds are more heavily weighted in favour of the questioner. Most of us will be fortunate enough never to experience these but we may read about them in the writings of those who have been in the hands of the police in countries where brain-washing is practised on political suspects. In this situation, the questioner is not merely given authority by prestige; he may also have the power to keep the questioned person in prison, to torture him, and perhaps to end his life. The suggestibility of the person questioned may be increased by prolonged questioning, by being made to stand for many hours, by deprivation of sleep, by anxiety or by drugging. We may well doubt whether mere psychological understanding of the process would enable one in the end to resist its effects even though such understanding might be helpful in the early stages.

Some people are, however, more resistant to such situations than others. The accounts given by the more resistant suggest that the preservation of an attitude of emotional non-involvement is an important element in resistance. By emotional non-involvement is meant not responding to the questioner's anger by anger, or to his kindness with gratitude. Some have reported that they can maintain this emotional non-involvement by persisting in an attitude of contempt for their questioners; some by the harder but perhaps more effective device of persisting in an attitude of love towards them.

There may be no complete solution of the problem of how resistance to suggestion can be effected under such extreme conditions. It may be that for most of us, the situation of being brain-washed would be one in which the forces of irrationality would win. The moral would seem to be that our efforts should be directed towards preventing such situations from arising. We must resolve to maintain a form of government which does not use or need such methods. We should steadily resist political change in the direction of a police state, whether of the right or of the left.

We were talking earlier of prestige suggestion based on false credentials. It may have better foundations and yet be harmful. Titles, offices of distinction, and university degrees are all authentic props to prestige but they can all be abused. One who has mastered a subject can claim a certain amount of reasonable authority in it. If a distinguished physicist expresses an opinion on a controversial physical topic, we may reasonably accept this opinion on his authority although we are not able ourselves to follow the reasoning that led to it. We can do this, not only because the speaker is in an academic position that implies a special knowledge of the topic under discussion, but also because there are other physicists who can follow his reasoning and check whether he is right or wrong. If, however, the physicist gives his opinion on the merits of socialism or the freedom of the human will, we should give his opinions only the respectful consideration we should give to those of any other intelligent person in possession of the same facts. We should certainly not quote his pronouncements as authoritative.

Let us call an argument based on the kind of authoritative statement which depends merely on the prestige of the speaker an 'appeal to mere authority', contrasting it with an appeal to reasonable authority. There was a time when the commonest argument in intellectual dispute was the appeal to mere authority, and it was considered sufficient to support a statement by saying: 'Aristotle said so-and-so', without considering whether Aristotle had a better reason for saying what he did than we have for saying the opposite. Still, some of us are content to settle disputed questions by appealing in exactly the same way to the authority of Marx, of St Paul, or even of the latest speaker we have heard at a lecture.

At one time the commonest appeal to mere authority was

an appeal to the opinion of the past. 'So-and-so has always been believed' was considered to be sufficient proof that the statement in question was true. Now we are more inclined to place authority in the opinions of the present and to regard 'So-and-so is believed by the modern man' as sufficient reason for accepting it as true. In all such cases we should not be hoodwinked by mere authority, but ask in the first case whether, in this particular matter, our ancestors had sound reasons for their opinion, and in the second case whether the modern man is in this matter better informed than his fathers and therefore more likely to be right. It is obvious that the modern man is more likely to be right in his opinion on such questions as the nature of the nebulae and the ways in which the different forms of animal and vegetable life have changed in the course of evolution, since many new facts have been discovered in these fields. It is not so obvious that the modern man is in a better position than his ancestors to come to right opinions on questions of religion and morals. Yet it is on such questions that he is particularly liable to be quoted as an authority. While reasonably grounded authority can be a force of great value as protection against the cruelties of commercial exploitation by humbug and quackery, yet it has been too often in the past a force opposing new thinking.

The prestige of professors and learned men has been used to oppose many movements of scientific discovery at their beginning. The authoritative voice of the learned world put off the acceptance of Harvey's discovery of the circulation of the blood for a whole generation. Lister's life-saving discovery of the use of antiseptics in surgery was similarly opposed by medical authority when it was first made. More recently, the prestige of established authority thundered against the revolutionary psychological discoveries of the great Austrian psychotherapist Freud. In the same way, when Professor Rhine confirmed the findings of previous students of telepathy that the mind could acquire knowledge without the use of the senses and even make correct reports of events that lay in the future, a great many psychologists were content to condemn his experimental results merely by the use of their authority, without trying to repeat them or to study his work.

One must, of course, bear in mind that authority has something to be said on its side. Not all novel ideas in any branch of science turn out to be of value; the innovator often turns out to be chasing a will-o'-the-wisp. So it is not unreasonable for those with experience in some branch of learning to say: 'We have seen what looked like bright new ideas turning out to be mistakes. This new suggestion is one which our experience of the subject leads us to expect to be a fruitless one.' Often they will be right; occasionally they will be disastrously mistaken. In any case, it is a reason not for rejecting a new idea but for taking a cautious attitude at the beginning and subjecting it to rigid testing before it is accepted as true. But where the prestige of authority has been used in an attempt to stifle new ideas, it has not been on any such reasonable ground as this. Rather the authorities have said in effect: 'As authorities on this subject, we know, without any detailed examination, that this is absurd.'

Already, I think, prestige suggestion is beginning to lose its force, and the pronouncements of 'authorities' now meet with more critical intelligence and less humble acceptance than was once the case. I have heard a professor deplore the fact that modern students no longer reverence their professors. God forbid that they should! It is part of the business of a professor to see that his students remain in a condition of critical alertness towards what he tells them instead of falling into this reverence which is the emotion accompanying the acceptance of prestige suggestion. The best teachers are not those who use their prestige to force meek acceptance of what they say, but those who retain to the end of their days the spirit of students, always ready to learn more, and expecting, from those whom they have to teach, argument, contradiction, and above all, the impartial testing of the truth by experiment.

After we have said all we can against the use of tricks of suggestion, it remains true that, in public speaking, some devices will be used that are liable to lead to the influence of suggestion on the audience. If anyone is giving a public address and decides, in the interests of straight thinking, that he will not speak in a confident voice and never make any point more than once, he will not be a success as a speaker. His audience will be bored and are more likely to be impressed with his incompetence than with his honesty. It would not even be practicable for a speaker to get rid of all prestige effects by persuading his chairman to tell the plain truth about his complete lack of competence to make any worthwhile contribution to the subject he is speaking on.

We should do all we can to reduce suggestibility by directing education towards independence of judgement and by showing the hollowness of the greater number of prestige pretensions, but when we come to speak in public we must address our audience firmly and confidently, using the method of varied repetition and under the protection of so much of a halo of prestige as the chairman sees fit to provide us with.

We should do this not in order that we may exploit the suggestibility of our audience, but because it is the only efficient way of public speaking. Suggestion, however, will follow whether we intend it or not; our audiences will tend to accept what we say to them quite independently of any reasonable ground for supposing it to be true. Intellectual honesty makes therefore, certain demands on a public speaker. He must never say in a public speech what he would not be prepared to maintain in private argument. He must not put forward as certain a statement which he thinks is only probably true. He must never use the politician's common trick of crushing an honest objector by a dishonest reply with nothing but tricks of suggestion to support it.

Intellectual honesty is not necessarily incompatible with public speaking, and there is no reason why those who value intellectual integrity should leave all the public speaking of the world to be done by the tricksters and the exploiters of suggestibility. Yet the atmosphere of the public platform is not favourable to intellectual honesty, and there is every reason why a public speaker should examine his conscience carefully in the light of what he knows about the mechanism of suggestion. His best protection, however, is an alert, critical, and relatively unsuggestible audience, fully aware of the nature of tricks of suggestion and of the difference between such tricks and honest arguments.

CHAPTER X

HABITS OF THOUGHT

THE LAST chapter dealt with the force of suggestion by which other people may act on our minds to make us less rational. There are also forces within our own minds that tend to produce crooked thinking. Two of these are our habits of thought and our prejudices. These are two different forces of a somewhat similar kind. I am using the term 'habits of thought' for those directions which our thoughts normally and habitually take, and 'prejudices' for those ways of thinking which are predetermined by strong emotional forces in their favour, by self-interest (real or supposed), by social involvements with one's own or alien groups, and so on. Both habits of thought and prejudices may be exploited by propagandists in somewhat similar ways.

The formation of habits of thought is part of the familiar process of habit-formation in our lives. Our daily life is largely directed by habitual ways of behaving; we get up, eat breakfast, and go to work in much the same way each day. Such habit-formation has the psychological value of economizing effort; choice is arduous and may conveniently be reserved for decisions of importance. The same is true with respect to our ways of thinking and forming opinions. When we read our newspapers, we read news items about race problems in South Africa, about violent demonstrations here and there, about differences of opinion between the governments of the USA and Russia, and so on. We have most likely already made up our minds about the rights and wrongs of all of these problems before (or we may have had our minds made up for us) so we need not form new opinions about them. Our thought-habits avoid the necessity for making new decisions on the controversial issues underlying these news reports. This economizing of intellectual effort is a principal advantage of having formed thought-habits.

There are, on the other hand, at least two grave disadvantages of thought-habits. First, knowledge of his hearers' thought-habits can be used as a weapon by the propagandist. Secondly, thought-habits may have the tendency to close our minds to new ideas.

The public speaker who wishes to exploit the thought-habits of his hearers will generally know enough about his audience to find no great difficulty in starting off his speech with some statements which exactly fit those thought-habits. He knows when he has succeeded in doing this by the applause which follows. A skilful orator may begin his speech with a succession of such statements. He refers to 'the British traditions of justice and fair play' (applause), to 'the sturdy common sense of the British people' (more applause), and to 'the unconquerable spirit of our race' (still more applause). By this time he has produced in his audience an attitude of willingness to accept what he says. He can now go on to say things which earlier their thought-habits would have led them to reject. He can say, for example, that our grandmotherly social legislation is turning the country into a soup-kitchen, or that the glory of our Commonwealth is being dimmed by our idleness or drunkenness. And the audience go on accepting what he says. The resistance which would certainly have been shown against these statements if he had started with them has been broken down by this simple device of beginning with easily accepted statements.

The same device may be used by a quack psychological

healer. He tells his audience that the mind has great power over the body, which is true. He goes on to illustrate this power by stories which may also be true. He may tell, for example, of people who seemed to be dumb or paralysed who became suddenly well under the influence of some emotional crisis. He may even illustrate this power by some simple experiments. When his audience are in a receptive state of mind he goes on to tell them other things which, without this preparation, they would have found less easy to believe. He may tell them that he has a new method by which all their illnesses, physical and mental, may be cured, which method will be communicated to small groups on payment of a fee. If this device of softening-up by preliminary appeal to habits of thought has succeeded, the members of the audience will have gone on believing the speaker when he has made these unsupported claims because the first things he said seemed to them to be obviously true. They will then be poorer by the amount of the fee and they may be no better in health.

So if we hear a succession of statements A, B, C, and D, which our minds accept readily and with enthusiasm, we must still be on our guard against accepting a fifth statement, E. A, B, C, and D may only have been ground-bait intended to produce the habit of swallowing everything the speaker says; E may conceal the hook.

Our caution, however, should extend even further than this. The ease and readiness with which we accept A, B, C, and D is no guarantee that even they are true. Thoughts we have often thought pass through our minds with increasing ease until they appear obvious. Emotions that have been called up in connection with particular thoughts are aroused more easily by those thoughts until the connection between emotion and thought appears to us to be a necessary one. So an appreciation of psychology should lead us to reject the old philosophical axiom that what we cannot doubt must be true. What we cannot doubt may simply be based on a very deeply rooted thought-habit and may well be false.

Our ancestors, for example, found themselves unable to doubt that the earth stood still while the sun moved round it every day. We ourselves may have found it equally difficult to doubt that there is an exact meaning in the statement that two events in different places occurred at the same time. Yet both of these convictions were wrong, and were based simply on deeply grounded habits of thought. One of these sets of thought-habits was broken by Copernicus when he showed that the facts were better explained by supposing that instead of the sun moving round the earth, the earth rotated on its axis. The other set was broken by Einstein when he revolutionized physics by bringing forward his special theory of relativity.

We all have a newspaper acquaintance with Einstein's theory of relativity, so I can safely take from it another example of the power of thought-habits to hinder the mind from reaching new truth. In his general theory of relativity, Einstein made a statement offensive to our 'common sense' (that is, to our habits of thought) by saying that space in the neighbourhood of matter was non-Euclidean. This means that in such space the angles of a triangle would not add up to two right angles.

Now the proposition that the three angles of every triangle together make up two right angles is a proposition in Euclid, but Euclid himself recognized that the proposition was a peculiar one. It was essential to nearly everything he proved afterwards, but itself rested on another proposition which could not be proved. So he treated this as an axiom, although it was not self-evident. Other geometers since Euclid's time have tried to prove this proposition, but no sound proof has been found, and it was finally decided that a sound proof was impossible. So other mathematicians worked out what they called 'non-Euclidean geometries', based on the assumption that the sum of the angles of triangles were less or were more than two right angles. If we make either of these assumptions, we can base a whole geometry on it. Such a geometry may not be true of the space we know, but it will be self-consistent. It will be true of a possible space, if not of the space in which we live.

Now it might be asked: 'What is the good of that kind of speculation? If we know that the angles of triangles do add up to two right angles what is the good of assuming they don't?' The answer was: 'The question is not whether they *do* add up to two right angles but whether they *must*. If they must, then the conclusions of Euclid would hold for all possible universes, but if it only happens that they do, and our conviction that they must has no better foundation than our habits of thought, then it is quite worth while to find out what are the consequences of the opposite assumption.' The important practical result of these speculations was that they made possible the acceptance of Einstein's theory (which was true and which had verifiable practical consequences). If people had remained convinced that every triangle must obey Euclid's law they could not have reached the general theory of relativity. Insight into new truth was made possible by the destruction of an old thought-habit.

Few of the thought-habits we may be asked to question will ever appear so obvious to us as the conviction that Euclidean geometry must be true. The apparent obviousness of a conviction is no guarantee of its truth. Once we are convinced of that, we should be prepared boldly to experiment in questioning the apparent truths based on our habits of thought.

The physical theory of relativity is a very useful example of the danger of thought-habits closing our minds to new truth, for it is in the fact of relativity in its wider sense that this danger is greatest. We all of us tend to judge problems from one particular standpoint – the one determined by our own conditions of life. We are inhabitants of our own particular country, with a particular religious and moral tradition, and we are inclined to forget how many of our judgements are simply relative to this single standpoint and are not absolute.

It is only when we begin to study comparative religions and comparative codes of morals that we begin to see to what extent our own opinions about right and wrong and about other matters are not scientific truths (for these are true for all persons under all conditions), but are judgements whose truth is relative to the particular point of view from which they were made. By accustoming our minds to comparative studies and by forming the habit of trying to look at problems in a manner which discounts our own point of view, we can to some extent escape from this relativity.

There is a story of many years ago about the captain of a British warship who was commissioned to visit a South Sea island and to make a report on the manners and customs of its inhabitants. His report is said to have been in some such terms as the following: 'The inhabitants of this island have no manners; as for their customs, they are beastly.' It is not difficult to see that this is not an objective account but one that is relative to the system of manners and customs the captain was accustomed to. It might be re-worded: 'Neither the manners nor the customs of the islanders were such as I should expect on my own quarter-deck.' A modern anthropologist would probably have discovered that the islanders had a very elaborate code of manners, and he would have recorded their customs as facts, without concerning himself with the question of which of them he liked and which he did not.

When people visit foreign countries, their reports are often of the same kind as this captain's. 'The South Europeans are dirty', 'The French eat queer foods', or 'The X people have no sense of humour'. Objectively considered, all these are statements in relation to our own customs as a frame of reference. The first states (truly or falsely) that South European people have a greater tolerance in some respects of matter in the wrong place than the traveller's own people have. The second states that the French eat different foods from those he is used to. The third means either that the X people laugh less than the traveller himself does, or (more probably) that they laugh at different things.

Particularly in international affairs we must remember this relativity of our point of view. If there were a dispute between, let us say, Bolivia and Peru, most of us would be able to judge its merits, if we had a sufficient knowledge of the facts, in an objective and scientific manner. If the dispute is, however, between our own and some other country, we can no longer do so. Until we can see and feel the other side's case as well as our own, our judgements cannot possibly even approach scientific validity. Most people seem not to realize this, and after a war we suppose that we and our allies are capable of acting not merely as prosecuting attorneys against our late enemies, but also as their judges. Now, a judge has to make objective, universally true judgements, and this could plainly only be done by someone as detached from our dispute as we should be from one between Bolivia and Peru.

An instructive experiment is to take a statement expressing our own point of view on a subject on which we have well-developed thought-habits; then, making no other alteration, to change the particular matters with which it deals to others which are similar but about which we have different thought-habits. Now we can consider the statement with its new subject-matter and see whether our attitude towards it remains the same. So we judge how far our attitude towards the original statement possessed objective or scientific validity, and how far it was acceptable to us merely because it fitted in with our thought-habits.

We may try this experiment with the following passage

from a speech which I found by chance at the back of a press-cutting. It is a stirring passage, so it is a suitable subject for an experiment to determine how much of its stir (if any) is independent of the thought and emotional habits it arouses:

Unless we play our part as an Imperial race there is nothing but disaster in front of the human race. (Applause.) With the effervescence that is going on in the world today, the only force to my mind which can maintain the ideal of ordered freedom is the 70 million, or thereabouts, of the white race of the British Empire, and the 70 million of the true American nation. These 140 million people, speaking the English tongue, reading the English Bible and the English Shakespeare, with ideas which were embodied originally in Magna Carta – these people with a common background of civilization have to share the responsibility for maintaining civilization among the 1800 or 1900 million people on the globe.

This is still a stirring speech, a little less so perhaps than when it was first delivered since our thought-habits have changed. We no longer so easily think of ourselves as the ideal bearers of civilization and order to the rest of the world. But if we remember that this was a common way of thinking in the early part of the present century, it is not difficult to understand why the speech won applause when it was delivered. Even now our thought-habits may not be so changed that it has lost all power to move us. So to test the real worth of this passage we will try it again in a setting in which we have formed different habits.

Let us suppose that Hitler had in 1939 made some such speech as the following:

Unless we Germans play our part as an Imperial race there is nothing but disaster in front of the human race.

With the effervescence that is going on in the world today, the only force to my mind which can maintain the ideal of ordered freedom is the 70 million, or thereabouts, of the Aryan peoples of Germany and the 5 million of true Germans living in Austria. These 75 million people, speaking the German language, reading the German Bible and the German Goethe, with ideas inherited from our Nordic ancestors – these people with a common background of civilization have to share the responsibility for maintaining civilization among the more than 2000 million people on the globe.

That is the same passage as before in a different setting. The setting has been changed to one in which we have different thought-habits. Our reaction, too, is different. Instead of a dignified statement of imperial responsibility, it sounds like an expression of national megalomania. How would the original passage have sounded to an impartial visitor from Mars?

One of the most important practical problems in which failure to see the situation from any other point of view than one's own may have disastrous consequences is in the genesis of quarrels. When these quarrels are on an international scale they may have the tragical consequence of war. In some respects their mode of origin may not be very different from the more trivial quarrels between individuals.

Let us suppose that Mr Jones finds the cat of his neighbour Mr Robinson scratching up the seed-beds in his garden. He writes a note of protest to Mr Robinson. Mr Robinson resents the note and sends an unconciliatory reply. Mr Jones is still more annoyed by this and puts wire-netting between the gardens, fastening it to the fence (which fence happens to be the property of Mr Robinson). Mr Robinson is angered by this disfigurement of his fence and cuts the wire-netting off. Mr Jones then sues Mr Robinson for damage to his wire-netting, while Mr Robinson sues Mr Jones for damage to his fence.

We now have a fully developed quarrel. The point of view of each participant is that his neighbour became aggressive on trivial grounds while he himself merely took action to protect himself. If the disputants appeal to us, as impartial onlookers, to decide which was the aggressor, we shall find it difficult to decide. We may prefer to say that both have found themselves in a peculiar situation in which their mutual hostility is intensified by each step taken. We may also judge that both are to blame because the grounds of the quarrel were so trivial that either might properly have broken the chain of increasing instability by refusing to take the defensive step which acted as the provocation to the next defensive step taken by his neighbour. If such a quarrel had started in the nursery, it would probably have been settled before it went very far by both antagonists being smacked and sent to bed.

A very parallel situation may arise between two nations. Nation X may fear the danger of war with nation Y, so X decides to increase the strength of its armed forces. Y sees in this a threat to its security and increases its own armed forces. X is confirmed in its impression that Y intends to make war and increases its own forces, also making a treaty for mutual defence with a neighbouring country, Z. Y is now sure of X's aggressive intentions and feels that it is beginning to be encircled by enemies, so it builds more tanks, aeroplanes and ships and makes alliances with its neighbours so that it can have additional forces for its protection, new airfields, etc. At the same time, the statesmen of both nations assure the world of their sincere desire for peace and the reluctance with which they are engaged in war preparations in order to protect themselves against the aggressive intentions of the other nation.

From the point of view of X, the position is simply that Y

is preparing for war and that they are merely taking steps to defend themselves. From the point of view of Y, X is threatening war while they themselves are preparing to resist X's aggression. From the point of view of a neutral observer, the situation may be parallel to that of Mr Jones and Mr Robinson, that both find themselves in a peculiar situation in which any defensive step taken by either is interpreted by the other as a threat, itself leading to another step of the same kind, which in its turn is regarded as a threat.

The situation is one of increasing instability, which at any point may really precipitate a war. The unstable equilibrium may indeed be upset at an early stage of the process if either X or Y, being convinced that the other nation intends to have a war at some time, also feels that the chance of their own defeat will be greater next year than now, so the war had better start now.

Unfortunately the chain of causes leading to war is less easy to break than in the case of Mr Jones and Mr Robinson, for the issue is not a trivial one. If a statesman of X fails to take steps to counter what he regards as provocative measures by Y, and if war does nevertheless break out between X and Y, a heavy weight of blame will rest on him for not having taken steps necessary to guard against the defeat of his country. It may be argued that it is better that he should risk defeat than that he should risk war. This may be true; it must obviously depend partly on the relative amounts of the two risks, and that is a difficult matter for him to judge. In any case, his decision is a difficult one. He has to weigh against each other the danger that he may provoke war by defensive measures which the other side regards as provocative and that he may risk defeat by neglecting those measures.

The pressure of his own nationals is likely to be altogether on the side of taking the measures which seem provocative to Y, because his people (and he himself) will see the situation from the point of view of his own nation X, which regards X as desiring peace and Y as aggressive. It is only if the statesmen and people of both X and Y can so far break their own habits of thought as to see the problem from the point of view of the other nation as well as their own that such a dangerous set of causes leading to war can be broken.

If states of hostility between nations are more difficult to bring to an end than those between neighbours quarrelling about their pets, it is also more necessary that they should be ended because of the ever-increasing danger of a major war with modern weapons leading to an irretrievable disaster to the human race. So those who try to look at international tensions from a point of view different from that of their own national interests are doing a real service to mankind. International misunderstanding is continually being intensified by patriotic talk and oratory on both sides of every pair of nations in a situation of mutual quarrel. The people of the world are still far from such a degree of clear thinking that they can look at the problems of other nations as if they were their own. The development of a capacity for such thinking would give us a protection against war better than any that can be provided by the increased fear of war through the making of more deadly weapons.

This is one field in which the questioning of our habits of thought may lead to a clearer insight into the nature of a situation with greatly increased chance of our behaviour being reasonable. In general, our thought-habits are not to be passively accepted but subjected to critical scrutiny. Even the things about which we feel most certain have been questioned, and it may not be a bad thing for us to hear these questionings, so that our deepest beliefs may be based on reasoned and critical conviction and not merely on thought-habits. One may, for example, profitably read newspapers and books representing a political point of view which is not one's own.

A Christian believer may read what is said against Christianity by such critics as Nietzsche and Bertrand Russell. One who is conservative in politics may read the writings of Marx or Kropotkin or Mao. One whose political thought is inclined to liberalism may read what is said on the other side by the conservative press or by speakers of the right. Those who believe in the institution of marriage as standardized in our culture may read what Germaine Greer says about it.

These will all experience the uncomfortable sensation of having their long-held and deeply ingrained thought-habits shaken. Their opinions may not be reversed, but they will no longer be merely based on thought-habits which have never been questioned. They will be something stronger and better, the reasoned convictions of free minds. Those whose attitude towards what they regard as subversive literature and speech is simply that it must be suppressed (by force if necessary) show little faith in the reasonableness of the beliefs they are so anxious to protect.

We have in ordinary speech a word for the unpleasant feelings that are aroused in us when something presented to us breaks across cherished mental habits. We say we are 'shocked'; and we resent being shocked. Many people believe in a censorship of plays, books, films, and wireless talks which will save them from any danger of being shocked. They avoid reading books or going to plays which may shock them. Those of our fathers who were most tender to their thought-habits avoided reading such writers as Ibsen and Shaw because they thought that these authors were deliberately trying to shock them. They do not seem particularly shocking to us, because they succeeded in their aim of shaking people's thought-habits so well that the ideas they suggested are no longer startling, but familiar. Some seem to us to be true and some false, but all such as may be thought about and talked about without any discomfort.

We can get the same profit by reading more modern authors who seem at first sight to be merely perversely questioning what every sensible person knows to be true. Such writers do us a great service (the service done to the science of physics by the writers on non-Euclidean geometry), of forcing us to question our old beliefs, so that we may freely and intelligently choose what is sound in them and reject the rest, and thus have our minds prepared for seeing new and unfamiliar truths. Most people do not need protection from being shocked. They need to be shocked a great deal more than they are.

This is probably more generally recognized now than it was when I first wrote *Straight and Crooked Thinking*. At any rate, now in the seventies, there is more writing that gives shocks than there was earlier in the century, and the implied questioning of generally accepted habits of thought is more thorough-going than it used to be. It is, however, still the case that those who value settled ways of thinking exert pressure for censorship of the more shocking kinds of literature. There can, of course, be a reasonable case for prohibiting the printing of some writings but not on the ground that they would shock some readers. A better ground for preventing the publication of a book is that the reading of it would lead to evil behaviour. Whether or not this would be the result of reading a particular book is not easy to judge, and the grounds on which it would be judged are different from those that would be used for determining whether a book is shocking. There are, for example, some four-letter words of Anglo-Saxon derivation describing sexual and excretory functions which are generally avoided in polite conversation. Their use in a book undoubtedly shocks some of its readers, but there does not seem to be any reason for supposing that their behaviour will be affected by having read them. On the other hand, there is a much stronger case against the literature of cruelty and a considerable probability that the reading of it may produce evil effects in behaviour. It remains true, I think, that the rational grounds of censoring the publication of any material must be its expected influence on behaviour and not the fact that it shocks people.

The value of shocks administered in literature lies in the fact that there are a number of problems about which most people have so many habits of thought that they resent any questioning of them. 'Is the institution of monogamous marriage a satisfactory one, or should changes be made in it? If changes should be made, how drastic are these to be?' 'Should the size of families be regulated in such a way as to produce zero population growth?' 'What social provision should be made for those who love members of their own and not of the opposite sex?' 'Is it better that the greater part of the wealth of the country should be in the possession of individuals or of the state?' 'Is it a glorious thing to fight and die for one's country?' These are all questions which merely to raise in public is to set in action thought-habits connected with such strong emotions that reasonable discussion and reasonable decision are quite impossible. Yet there should be no question reasonable people dare not ask, no thought so shocking that we cannot consider it long enough to make a sensible decision as to whether it is true or false.

We must not suppose that we have escaped the danger of being imprisoned by our thought-habits merely by giving up our old habits of thought which are much the same as everybody else's and starting new ones of our own. The unorthodox and unconventional are in just as much danger of finding their minds closed to new truth by the persistence of their old habits of thought as are the orthodox and the conventional. They too have just the same need of being occasionally shaken out of their thought-habits so that they may retain flexibility of mind.

A danger which threatens those who have rejected commonly accepted habits of thought is that they should form the habit of disbelieving things merely because other people believe them. They then become what are commonly called 'cranks'. A crank is not an individual free from thought-habits, but one who has formed a system of thought-habits which is likely to be as hampering to him as is the opposite system of habits of accepting all that is commonly believed.

It should be one of the aims of education to produce a quality that we may describe as 'flexibility of mind', an ability to try out new ways of thinking and to make unfamiliar assumptions. This means that we must be able at will to put on one side our old thought-habits. The mathematicians had thought-habits based on the fact that the angles of all the triangles they had ever met had added up to two right angles, but they were able to ask themselves: 'Suppose they hadn't, what would follow?' So we must keep for ourselves the power of intellectual experimentation. We see everywhere men carrying out work for wages or salary. We must ask ourselves: 'Is this a necessary law, or can we imagine a form of society in which the monetary motive would not be the dominant one and yet in which the world's work would be done?' We are accustomed to a particular form of marriage relationship. We should ask ourselves: 'Is this the only one possible? Would other kinds of relationship be better or worse in securing the ends for which marriage exists?' We have probably been brought up in a particular religious tradition whose teachings may seem to us to be self-evidently true. It may, nevertheless, be profitable to try the experiment of thinking ourselves into some other system of religious belief, so that we can go some way towards seeing with the eyes and hearts of those holding a different system of beliefs, which may be not merely those of some other Christian denomination but perhaps of some other religion, such as Buddhism or Islam. Such an exercise may not change our own beliefs; it should change our attitude towards those who hold other systems of belief.

Clearly it is neither desirable nor possible to get rid of all thought-habits. The formation of thought-habits is as inevitable as the formation of bodily habits and just as useful. But we must be ready continually to revise them. Thought-habits once serviceable may prevent us from attaining to new truths. We differ from the lower animals in the possession of a rich and complicated brain. This is an instrument to give flexibility and adaptability to our behaviour. If we allow ourselves merely to become creatures of habit, we become automatic and mechanical like the lower animals. We are allowing our brains to degenerate into mere mechanisms when they were meant for plasticity and change.

Astronomers tell us that the human race has many million years more to spend on this globe if it does not destroy itself by war, environmental pollution, or unrestricted population growth. It is only by flexibility of mind that we can continue to adapt ourselves to an ever-changing environment. Inflexibility of mind may lead to the extermination of the human race.

CHAPTER XI

PREJUDICE

HABITS OF thought are not the only internal factors that predispose us to crooked thinking. There are also our prejudices, already defined as the ways of thinking that are predetermined by strong emotional forces such as those derived from our own self-interest or by our social involvements. These may have the effect of making us unwilling to think straight on certain topics. Someone who has never heard of the laws of logic may come to quite correct conclusions on such a question as the relative chances of drawing a red and a black card by a chance draw from a complete pack, where the facts are simple and the reasoning perfectly straightforward. On the other hand, the learned author of a textbook on logic may be quite unable to come to correct conclusions on a question in which his own interests are deeply involved – such a question, for example, as the economic justification of a kind of taxation which bears hardly on himself.

Education does not in itself save us from this disability. It ought to help us in the direction of freedom from prejudice, but it does not necessarily do so. Learned men are often as bound by their prejudices as anyone else. The learned man may defend his most unreasonable prejudices by arguments in correct logical form while the uneducated man defends his by illogical arguments. The difference is plainly not much to the advantage of the learned man. The fact that he can marshal formally correct arguments in defence of his errors may make these more watertight against opposing arguments and against opposing experience. His mastery of the art of thought may simply make his unreasonable opinions more unassailable.

Of course, you, being free from his prejudices, may see the flaw in his reasons for holding the opinions, but this flaw may very well not be in the form of his arguments. It may lie in what he assumes, or in what facts he selects of all possible facts to consider. I do not wish to suggest that correct thinking on correct facts can lead to error, but only that there are other routes to error than lack of logic, and the most logical mind guided by its prejudices can and will find its way to error by one of these other routes.

There was an old opinion (still commonly current) that the lunatic is a person suffering from a defect in his power of reasoning. Now no general statement about lunatics is likely to be true because the term 'lunacy' covers many different kinds of mental disorder. The kind of mentally disordered person generally meant in this statement was the *paranoiac*, whose main symptom is that he holds some absurd belief, such as that he is the incarnation of some long-dead monarch, or that a group of other persons are engaged in a conspiracy against him. In other words, he suffers from *delusions*.

If we actually meet a paranoiac and discuss with him his belief that he is a reincarnation of Napoleon, of Julius Caesar, or of Jesus Christ, we do not find a loss of reasoning power. On the contrary, he reasons most persistently about the very subject of his delusions, and the quality of his reasoning is determined by his intellectual development. If he has a keen, logical intellect he will reason keenly and logically. He will apply the same standard of reasoning in defence of his delusions as he would, if he were sane, apply to the defence of his sane opinions. This standard may be high; it may be low. Even sane persons have often a somewhat low standard of reasoning. Ask the average man in the street why he believes that the world is round; he is likely to give you a set of very bad reasons. Ask the believer in the delusion that the earth is flat why he holds this belief, and he will probably give you a much better set, for his reasoning powers have been sharpened in continual controversy with people holding the orthodox view. Yet he is wrong and the illogical man in the street is right. The man with wrong opinions is not necessarily the worse reasoner.

In the same way, the person suffering from insane delusions may show no loss of reasoning power. His defect is that the opinions he holds are very badly wrong, and that his reasoning is used to support these wrong opinions and not to criticize them. Their source is not reasonable. They form a kind of super-prejudice.

When any of us hold the kind of opinions we have called 'prejudices', we have a part of our minds in a condition similar to that of the delusional system of the insane. We too reason to the best of our ability in defence of our prejudices, but these reasonings are not the real support for our opinions. These are based on other (often quite irrational) grounds.

If we argue directly against the false beliefs of a person suffering from delusional insanity, we shall find our arguments unable to shake his beliefs, because they are not directed against the real causes of those beliefs. The more successful of our arguments will, however, have a result dangerous to ourselves, for they may produce an explosion of violent anger. The deep-seated system of emotions protected so carefully by the set of false beliefs will also be protected by anger and physical violence if the protective system of beliefs is in any way threatened.

The same is true to a lesser degree of the opinions of a sane person grounded on emotional or practical needs. He will not willingly allow those beliefs so necessary to his mental comfort to be overthrown, and if our arguments begin to threaten them he will grow angry or at least peevish. When he begins to show anger instead of reasonable opposition to our arguments, we may press home our advantage, for this is an indication that his beliefs are beginning to be threatened by our arguments.

This use of an opponent's signs of anger as an indication that we have touched what he feels to be a weak spot in his argument is, of course, a perfectly legitimate device in argument. There is also a dishonest trick which may be used in connection with the anger of an opponent. This is the trick of deliberately angering him in order that we may take advantage of the fact that he will argue less efficiently in a condition of anger. This we may do, not only by pressing on a weak point in his argument, but also by adopting a deliberately offensive or insolent manner, by making fun of matters on which he obviously feels strongly, or by the use of such irritating tricks as diversion by irrelevant objection.

Knowledge of the nature of this trick and of its purpose makes the remedy obvious. We must always be determined that nothing shall make us angry in discussion, because, however annoying our opponent may be, we shall best defeat him by keeping our temper under control. If we feel anger arising, this should be a signal to be increasingly courteous to our opponent and increasingly critical of our own position. We can use the first stirrings of anger to detect the weaknesses of our own position as well as can our opponent.

We may express shortly the effect of prejudice on opinion by saying that we are inclined to believe what we either desire or need to be true and to disbelieve what we desire or need to be false. If we have put our last pound on a horse running at a hundred to one, we fervently believe that he will win and we shall hotly contest a friend's proposition that he cannot run and will most likely come in last. Similarly, if a man is suffering from a dangerous illness he tends to refuse to believe that his illness can really be fatal because his desire for life makes him unwilling to accept the evidence that he is unlikely to recover.

Sometimes it is obvious how the emotions which determine our acceptance of some propositions and rejection of others came into existence. Practically all men desire money and comfort, and fear ruin and death, so they will tend to accept propositions whose truth would secure their wealth, comfort, and security of living, and reject those whose truth would threaten them. We can see how general this law is when we notice how nearly universal is the rule that those who have possessions (even a few) are politically on the side of preservation of the existing order, while revolutionaries are, on the whole, recruited from the non-possessors.

Sometimes, however, the connection between emotions and prejudices is more obscure. The emotion lying behind a prejudice may be a relic of the emotional life of early childhood. Our childish love for our father or our resentment against his discipline may be the determining cause of our adult reverence for authority or of our rebellion against it. Which of these two factors was the stronger in our childhood may thus determine whether we shall be monarchists or republicans, conservatives or revolutionaries. Similarly, our sympathy with oppressed peoples may be based on our childhood's phantasies of rescuing our mother from distress.

Whether the connection between the prejudice and the emotion giving rise to it seems obvious, as in the case of political opinions determined by the amount of a man's possessions, or obscure, as in the case of opinions determined by his childhood relationship to his father, recognition of this connection may not be possible for the holder of the prejudice. It is the essential nature of a prejudice that the connection should not be apparent. The prejudiced person believes that he holds his opinion on entirely rational grounds. If he understood that his opinion was really based on irrational grounds, his prejudice would disappear. He might still hold his former opinion or he might reject it, but if he held it, it would have to be on other grounds than those on which it was based when it was a prejudice. The strength of the prejudice depends on the fact that he cannot become aware of these irrational grounds on which it is based. The further these grounds are hidden from his awareness, the more strongly is the prejudice held.

Let us suppose that two men are arguing about a proposal to levy a tax on all the capital held by an individual in excess of a certain amount. One of them is in favour of the levy. He argues the case in its favour entirely on general grounds, with logical arguments as to its general economic effects. His opponent argues hotly against it with equally general arguments. Neither of them argues the question from any consideration of how the proposal would affect him personally, and both would indignantly repudiate the suggestion that the effect of the levy on themselves plays any part in determining their opinions about it. Yet, as onlookers, we are not surprised to learn that the man arguing for the levy has no capital, while the man arguing against it owes much of the comfort of life to the interest on a capital sum either saved by himself or inherited. Nor are we likely to be wrong in guessing that these facts are much more important influences in determining the opinions of the two men than any of the logical arguments they bring forward so impressively.

Or we may look at the newspaper correspondence about a proposal to put a school for mentally deficient children or a rehabilitation centre for drug addicts in the residential district of Linden Avenue. Most of the letters which are critical of the proposal will find fault with it on general grounds: that the motor traffic along Linden Road would be dangerous for the school children, or that it would be disagreeable for the children of Linden Avenue to see handicapped children going past their houses or that it would be dangerous for them to have drug addicts in their neighbourhood. Other letters may support the proposal on the ground that it is good for handicapped children to have their education in a pleasant district or that the respectable environment of Linden Avenue is ideal for the rehabilitation of drug addicts. None mention personal reasons for objecting to or supporting the proposal, but when we look at the addresses from which the letters are written, we find that most of those objecting to the proposal are from people living on or near Linden Avenue, while the letters supporting the proposal come from other districts. We may well guess that the question of how much the writers of the letters will be personally affected by the proposal is a more important factor in determining their attitude towards it than the more general considerations which they bring forward as arguments.

We must not, however, make the mistake of supposing that, when opinions based quite irrationally on people's personal desires or repugnances are bolstered up by apparently reasonable arguments, this is simply hypocrisy in the ordinary sense. The holder of such an opinion is generally quite unconscious of the irrational grounds of his belief and honestly believes that his reasonable arguments are the real ground for his belief. He would be genuinely indignant if it were suggested that his opinions on the question under dispute had anything to do with a consideration of how he himself would be affected. The true reasons for his belief are hidden from his consciousness. He is not a hypocrite; he is merely a self-deceiver.

Such a rational bolstering up of a belief held on irrational grounds has been called a 'rationalization'. When our desires lead us to accept a belief, our minds construct an apparently rational set of reasons for supposing that belief to be true. The belief does not, however, follow from the reasons; the reasons follow from the belief. They are mere 'rationalizations' of a belief really held on irrational grounds. A sufficiently ingenious mind can rationalize any belief, however absurd. Some people can produce rationalizations for the belief that the British are the ten lost tribes of Israel, others for the belief that the world is flat, while others will defend fox-hunting on the ground that foxes like being hunted. The capacity of many people to deceive themselves by rationalizations is a formidable barrier to straight thinking.

There are other beliefs of this kind, intermediate between the delusional systems of the paranoiac and the prejudices of the normal person. An interesting example is to be found in the belief that the ratio between the circumference and the diameter of a circle (the quantity 'pi') can be expressed as an exact fraction or as a finite decimal. Books are written and societies are formed in support of this view although it can be demonstrated to be false. Yet the holders of this and similar views are not usually insane. They are abnormal in the fact that they hold these opinions with an irrational degree of certainty and that they show unusual imperviousness to opposing evidence. In these respects they resemble true paranoiacs but in other respects they do not. Such systems of thought may be called 'paranoid' systems, using the termination-*oid* to indicate that they are *like* paranoiac delusions.

If paranoid systems were only concerned with such topics as the flatness of the earth, the fate of the ten lost tribes of Israel, or the value of 'pi', they would be of no great practical importance, although they would remain interesting as illustrations of the strength of the irrational forces in human minds. They become serious when they take a form resembling the insane person's delusion of persecution. The typical form of such a paranoid system is: 'There is an enemy "X". He is cunning, powerful and wicked and his aim is to destroy our civilization. He is responsible for drug addiction, sexual perversion, strikes, student demonstrations and wars'. The unknown 'X' may be identified with some known group or it may be left somewhat vague. 'X' may be identified with the Jews, the Communists, the Freemasons, the Jesuits, or any combination of these. The mode of operation of 'X' may be regarded as a wide-spread though secret conspiracy of which the 'liberals' are considered to be unwitting collaborators.

A good example of such a paranoid system in which 'X' was identified with the Jews is to be found in Hitler's *Mein Kampf* which is now far enough away in time to be looked at objectively. One can recognize its quality of persuasiveness which led to wide-spread acceptance of its point of view in Hitler's own country. Yet the ground for its theory of a Jewish plot is no more than unsupported assertion in emotionally charged language. The alleged details of the plot were derived from a book called *The Protocols of the Elders of Zion* which is known to be a forgery. It is possible, of course, that Hitler himself was insane, a true paranoiac. But the paranoid system he evolved was accepted by millions of sane persons, and this acceptance produced terrible damage to the world and its peace.

The development of paranoid systems of thought of the persecutory type did not end with Hitler. In our own culture the enemy 'X' in such a system may be 'the reds' who are said to be responsible for student demonstrations, for high rates of taxation, and for sexual activities in universities. 'The Jews' or 'the Jesuits' may also be included in 'X'. I have myself received a pamphlet (in Australia) which referred to the discredited *Protocols of the Elders of Zion* as evidence of a Jewish world plot, and even claimed that the rise of Nazism in Germany was part of that plot.

It is desirable that those who value a rational approach to political, racial and religious questions should be able to recognize the character of such paranoid propaganda when they meet it. For this purpose some understanding of the nature of paranoid systems is useful. There are, of course, reasonable arguments against the Communist system of government and reasonable Protestant arguments against the teachings of the Roman Catholic Church. But these reasonable cases are not promoted by delusions of Communist and Popish plots. These are part of crooked thinking and interfere with a rational assessment of the real issues.

Since it is an essential character of prejudice that its sources are hidden from consciousness, it might seem to be impossible for us to become aware of our own prejudices so that we may become free from their influence. It is hopeless to try to do so by looking inside our own minds and trusting we shall so be able to recognize our prejudices. Their source is hidden from our own consciousness and they will look to us just like rational beliefs. But we can learn to recognize them in another way – by applying to our own opinions the same criteria as we apply when we see prejudice in other people. If we see another man holding opinions that correspond to his wishes we suspect that these opinions are prejudices, and if we notice ourselves holding opinions that correspond to our own wishes we have equally good grounds for suspecting prejudice. If we find ourselves getting angry when some cherished belief is questioned, we may suspect that that belief is a prejudice based on irrational grounds just as we would if we observed another man unreasonably touchy about an opinion. We are not likely to understand fully the irrational sources of our opinions, but we can have some knowledge of them if we examine our own opinions as critically and unsympathetically as we do the opinions of others.

It is perhaps even more useful to keep a general awareness of the fact that we are likely to have prejudices and to adopt methods of counteracting their influence. One such influence, for example, is that they may lead us to overlook fallacious thinking in writings or speeches we agree with, while they enable us readily to detect errors in what we disagree with.

So, in all matters in which our emotions are strongly involved (either for or against), we must distrust our own judgements and compare them carefully with those of people who disagree with us. Our prejudices tend also to make us forget facts unfavourable to our opinions. Darwin records that he kept a notebook in which he jotted all facts or ideas which were opposed to his conclusions, because otherwise he forgot them. So it resulted that when he published his results, his opponents could bring forward few objections which he had not already considered himself.

One must be particularly cautious in quoting from memory any evidence in favour of a view one holds. I have frequently typed from an apparently vivid memory incidents recorded in books I had read, but on examining the books again before sending what I had written to be printed I have found the original passages were somewhat different from what I had quoted and were generally less favourable to the view I was trying to support. Serious errors of fact have crept in this way into books whose authors have not sufficiently realized how much memory may be distorted by prejudices.

There is a common fault in argument arising from the influence of prejudice which may be employed deliberately as a dishonest trick but which is more commonly used unwittingly by a speaker who is misled by his prejudices. This is the use in one context of an argument which would not be admitted in another context where it would lead to the opposite conclusion. This is 'special pleading'.

A Church dignitary, for example, who was actively engaged in trying to increase the stipends of poorly paid ministers, rebuked the coal-miners for wanting an increase of wages because 'a pound a week more wages does not mean a pound a week more happiness'. Receivers of large unearned incomes are heard to deplore the sapping of sturdy independence by the payments of insurance benefits to unemployed workers.

The construction of battleships is sometimes defended simply on the ground that it makes work – an argument which could equally well be used in defence of building roads in excess of requirements, making men shovel the sand from one point of our shore to another, or even (as Bernard Shaw pointed out) as an encouragement to motorists to knock down pedestrians. Obviously there can be reasonable arguments against an increase of miners' wages and against the payment of unemployment benefits, or in favour of the building of more battleships, but any such arguments can only be accepted if the principle on which they rest is applied to other particular cases as well as to the one under consideration.

In controversies about wages and salaries, one can hardly fail to notice how consistently some arguments are applied in one context and some in other. Captains of industry resist wage rises because of their inflationary tendency but they do not use this as an argument against increases of directors' fees which would seem also to be inflationary in their effect. Members of the more prosperous part of the community may argue that it is a good thing that they should have a large income because: (a) the amount they save increases the capital of the country, or because (b) the amount they spend, even on luxuries, is good for trade and increases employment. They may also argue that the wages of manual workers should be kept at a moderate level because: (c) the country cannot afford the burden of high wages, (d) poverty and hardship produce sturdy, manly characters, and (e) if the workers were paid more, they would only spend it on useless luxuries like colour television. There is obviously much special pleading here. (b) and (e) are inconsistent with one another; the view that luxury expenditure is socially valuable being applied to one class of the community while the view that it is a social evil is applied to another. (a) also is not applied to the manual workers, while (c) and (d) are not applied to the group to which the speaker himself belongs. We may further ask whether the person who argues in this way really believes (a) and (e), which imply that the thing of greatest social value to do with money is to save it, or (b) which implies that the right thing is to spend it on no matter what. It is useless to ask which he believes. He believes both propositions and will employ either in different contexts. Men have a much larger power of believing inconsistent propositions than is commonly supposed.

The obvious way to deal with special pleading is to get the person who is using this device to admit the general principle that underlies his particular argument and then to apply it to the particular cases he has ignored. A public speaker, for example, objected to proposed legislation for providing milk for poor children on the ground that it would make us a nation of milksops. One would need to ask the speaker whether all children who had a sufficiency of milk became milksops, which, if admitted, would lead to the further question, whether he would therefore deprive his own children of milk to ensure that they did not become milksops.

In trying to detect and undermine special pleading, one must be careful not to do one's opponent the injustice of attributing to him an extension (p 41) of his proposition. In the above case, for example, the speaker may not have intended to imply that all children tended to become milksops by drinking sufficient milk, but only the children of the poor, or only if the milk were provided by the community. We must allow him to tell us what the general proposition is that he is prepared to defend, and then attack it either by making other particular applications which he will reject, or by showing its untruth in some other way.

Knowledge of the prejudices of his audience can, of course, be used by an orator in exactly the same way as knowledge of their habits of thought. He can make easier the acceptance of a doubtful proposition by wording it in such a way as to make it appeal to the prejudices of his audience, or by introducing it only after the statement of a number of other propositions enthusiastically favoured by their prejudices. These devices and the methods of dealing with them are essentially the same as have already been described in the chapter on thought-habits, so they need not be dealt with here.

There is, however, a particular form of the first of these two devices which deserves fuller mention. That is the trick of commending or condemning a course of action because of its good or bad practical effects on the lives of one's hearers. A very considerable part of political propaganda is made up of this kind of appeal. Whether he is attacking national expenditure on armaments or on social services, a speaker can get a ready response by pointing to its effects in increased taxation. Our objection to increased taxation is primarily a very individual and personal one, that as we pay more in taxes we have less to spend on ourselves and our families. Even when the speaker makes a relatively impersonal basis to his appeal by emphasizing the effect of high taxation as a burden on industry, we can safely guess that it is the effect on themselves that his audience are thinking about. That is likely to be the true reason for the success of the speaker in carrying conviction.

Yet each of the audience could, if he were sufficiently detached emotionally from his own affairs, truthfully reflect that its effect on himself is not the wise ground for deciding on national policy. It is unimportant from the point of view of the community as a whole whether the ten pounds in his pocket is spent by himself or by the nation. Its expenditure by the nation will create as much employment as its expenditure by himself, and the important question is, which of the two ways of spending it will best promote the general good. In fact, he will not reason like this; an appeal to an audience to welcome with patriotic fervour a lowering of their own standard of living because this will benefit the nation as a whole is an appeal that falls very flat. It is a peculiarity of the sentiment of patriotism that men can be more easily persuaded to sacrifice their lives for their country than to sacrifice the contents of their pockets.

When people realize how many of their opinions and even of the reasoning processes by which these are supported are based on known or unknown emotional foundations, they may begin to doubt whether they can believe anything at all. This doubt is, of course, absurd. There must be right opinions even on questions about which the strength of our own feelings makes it most difficult to discover which they are. One way of distributing wealth can be better than another and rational thought can help to discover which is that better way even though his own possession or non-possession of wealth is likely to be the strongest influence in determining a particular individual's opinion as to which is the better way. Similarly, there must be an objectively true answer to the question whether at death we just disappear like candles blown out or whether we continue our conscious existence for all eternity. Yet which of us (whether believers or disbelievers in personal immortality) will suppose that he holds his opinions on the matter on grounds that are scientific and objective, and independent of his own feelings and desires?

The attitude of detachment of mind is one which can be cultivated and must be cultivated if we are to arrive at true conclusions on matters which touch us personally. The first step is to recognize the existence of this kind of irrational motivation in our own minds; then we can make allowances for it. If we are rich, we must try to force ourselves to think out social problems on general grounds without allowing ourselves to be influenced by our own powerful desire for the continuance of our own individual comfort and security. Whatever may be our individual circumstances, we must learn to adopt the same attitude towards the sorrows and pleasures of others as we do towards our own, and to adopt the same attitude towards our own sorrows and pleasures as we do towards those of other people. Of course, that is hard, much harder to do than to say. So we must always be prepared to admit that our conclusions as to what is best for others may have really been dictated to us by consideration of what is best for ourselves. But we can and must do our best to detach ourselves from our own irrational motivations of opinion. The first step in that detachment is to recognize them.

Nor must we make the foolish mistake of supposing that we can settle controversies by attributing prejudices to our opponents and by labelling their arguments 'rationalizations'. Some people seem to think that it is a sufficient argument against Socialism to say that it is based on the envy of those without possessions for those with, and that its intellectual defence is just a rationalization of this envy. This is no more reasonable than the opposite argument that Conservatism is merely based on the determination of the possessors to stick to what they have got, and that its intellectual defence is simply a rationalization of this determination. Undoubtedly the desire of the poor for wealth and of the wealthy for a continuance of their wealth are powerful motive forces behind the belief in Socialism and in Capitalism respectively. But having made all allowances for the strength of whichever of these prejudices our own circumstances have given us, the question remains – which is the better system? That is a question we cannot settle by discussing the prejudices of our opponents. A true opinion as well as a false one may owe much of its strength to irrational motives.

CHAPTER XII

PREDIGESTED THINKING

SOME OF the ways of crooked thinking which have been discussed are rooted in a characteristic of much human thinking which it will be worthwhile now to describe and name. Most true statements about complicated matters of fact cannot be adequately expressed in a few words. To give an account of the effect of diet or climate on health or of the effect of the imposition of a protective duty on an imported commodity would require many words, many qualifications, many distinctions between different cases, and many uncertainties. The majority of men will, however, have none of these complications. They feel that they have mastered the matter when they can reduce such a complicated question to a simple formula with all the qualifications, distinctions, and uncertainties left out. In the early years of the present century, a central issue at English parliamentary elections was the question of whether duty should be paid on various imported goods, including some that were used for food. The difficult and complicated problem of the effect of such duties on prices and employment was summed up in such phrases as 'Food taxes mean dear food' on the one side and 'Tariff reform means work for all' on the other.

Let us call this tendency 'predigested thinking'. We find it as a widespread reaction to intellectual complications. Darwin's complicated and beautiful theory of the evolution of organic life was popularly reduced to the simple formula: 'Men are descended from monkeys'. More recently Freud put forward the psychoanalytic theory of human emotional development which was a highly complicated and difficult body of doctrine. This, however, was very generally supposed to be adequately expressed by the formula: 'Everything is sex'. In the same way, the difficult mathematical physics of Einstein's theory of relativity may be summed up in the phrase: 'Everything is relative'. What dietetic research has discovered about the values of different kinds of food may also be summed up in predigested form as: 'Milk is nourishing', 'Jam contains calories', and 'Lettuces are full of vitamins'.

The tendency to eliminate complications from statements may explain the prevalence of the substitution of 'all' for 'some' (Chapter II), the occasional ignoring of the undistributed middle (pp 58–61), and the readiness to accept an extension of the position one starts to argue in favour of (pp 39–43). In all these cases, the substituted proposition is the less complicated one, and therefore the one that those under the influence of predigested thinking are liable to accept.

A man may, for example, be arguing against the teachings of Freud. He will almost certainly begin to attack the view that 'everything is sex'. His own tendency to predigested thinking has led him quite unwittingly to invite his opponent into the trap of the extension. His opponent may be better informed on the matter and try to explain which activities Freud thinks are related to sex and which he does not. This, however, is of no interest to the first speaker, and he escapes by protesting that his opponent is too 'learned' or too 'subtle' for him. He protests that he is a plain man and that nothing will convince him that art, romantic love, and religion are just sex, which is generally agreed by everybody to be the teaching of Freud. Thus he entrenches himself in his predigested thinking, and if the dispute takes place before an audience he can generally be sure of having their sympathy, for his opponent will seem to be a person trying to make himself out to be too clever and who makes serious argument impossible by throwing doubt on what everyone knows to be true.

The popular controversialist has indeed a serious complaint against those who do not accept the predigested thought formulae ordinarily current, because these are the agreed postulates for popular discussion. 'The Scots are a healthy race because they are bred on a diet of oatmeal', 'The Germans were responsible for both World Wars', 'The higher critics tried to prove that the Bible was not true, but their conclusions are now out of date', 'The welfare of a nation is based on the sanctity of its home life', 'The Socialists wish to reduce all men to a dull uniformity' – these are samples of the predigested postulates of newspaper controversy. Without them such controversy could not be carried on. Yet there is not one of them that can reasonably either be denied or affirmed: they are simple statements on a number of matters about which the truth could hardly begin to be told in less than several pages.

A statement expressed in predigested form has the great practical advantage that it can be easily remembered and easily passed from one person to another. It is, therefore, easy for belief in it to be increased by the force of 'suggestion' (Chapter IX). No kind of suggestion is stronger than the conviction that 'Everybody says so-and-so'. I was living in a village during an epidemic of influenza when word was passed from one back-garden to another: 'Bananas are so nourishing'. Neither proof nor authority was demanded. Whoever heard these words went off to buy bananas for those who were in bed. Apparently lettuces, breadcrumbs, or mushrooms could have been fitted into the formula with equal effect. This tendency to accept any predigested statement is being exploited by the advertiser who prints: 'Snooks's mixture cures your cold'.

A predigested thought formula expressed in a form of

words which is handed from one person to another may be called a 'slogan'. A successful slogan may possess great power in influencing the behaviour of a large number of people in one direction. No complicated statement of the doctrines of Rousseau could have been as effective in directing the French Revolution as the slogan 'Liberty, fraternity, equality'. Now, this slogan is obviously predigested. It is a very simple statement which would need a complicated expansion to mean anything exactly. Such an expansion of 'liberty' would need to explain what the people were and what they were not to be free to do; of 'fraternity', to explain with whom they were to be fraternal (not aristocrats or enemies of their country); of 'equality', in what respects they were to be equal. Yet such an expanded account would not serve any of the purposes of the slogan: that it should be readily accepted in its entirety, easily remembered, and able to stimulate a large number of people to similar action.

The use of slogans as a method of influencing people is not necessarily unreasonable. A skilful leader of men, however complicated were his own thought-processes, would need to express his doctrines in predigested form for them to be widely accepted, and, for the purposes of mass action, this could most conveniently be done by inventing slogans. Thus the Russian revolution was directed not by a preaching of the subtleties of Marx to the people, but by the slogan, 'All power to the Soviets'. This was a legitimate use of a slogan; slogans can reasonably and properly be used to stir people to action but not to induce belief.

Probably there is no single explanation of the tendency to accept and respond to predigested thinking. There is the difficulty of grasping a complex proposition. The most finely developed brain reaches at some point the limit of the complexity it can grasp. With the majority of men this limit is reached rather early. Long before it is reached, however,

mental idleness steps in, making us tend to accept mental food
well below the limits of our digestion. It is easier to believe
that Richard III or Hitler were thoroughly bad men than to
accept a dispassionate estimate of all the sides of their characters. So, through idleness or indifference, such a predigested
opinion is accepted even by those easily capable of making a
more complex judgement if they chose to make the necessary
mental exertion. We have also seen how easily predigested
thinking expressed in a slogan can be adapted for various
socially useful ends, as well as being convenient to remember.

There is, however, a much more important reason for the
acceptance of predigested thinking than these. It is that predigested thinking gives us a consistent practical attitude towards our life problems. During a war, for example, we are
inclined to think of our enemies as altogether evil, as treacher-
ous, murderous, and inhuman. This view was well expressed
by a newspaper correspondent during the Second World War:
'There are no poor dear German people . . . but only a brutal-
ized nation.' If, during a war, someone suggests that there is a
mixture of good and bad even in the enemy, or that some of
the stories of enemy atrocities may be exaggerated, or that
they have sometimes shown generous and humane behaviour,
he is regarded as a person of doubtful loyalty with a secret
sympathy for the enemy cause.

The feeling of outrage aroused by such an expression of
opinion is a result of the fact that its tendency is to undermine
the simplified picture of the enemy as evil, and therefore as
something which must be vigorously fought against. In a war,
one is engaged in the practical activity of fighting against the
enemy. Any belief which makes one fight more strenuously is
a serviceable one. From the same practical point of view any
belief which makes one fight less strenuously is undesirable.
The conduct of one's enemies, like the conduct of oneself, is,
in fact, mixed bad and good. But while belief in the bad

strengthens our hands in fighting, belief in the good side of our enemies' characters would weaken our fighting efforts. So we accept the over-simplified picture of our enemies as evil because that is the most useful picture for action, not because it is true.

Indeed, it is not only in wars and revolutions that one finds this kind of thinking in which all perfection tends to be attributed to one's own side and all evil to the enemy. In elections it is very noticeable; while the candidates on one side appear as models of all the civic and domestic virtues, those on the other are regarded as incompetent and untrustworthy persons. Here too action is required, and action must be simple although thought may be complex. One must vote on one side or the other: so to avoid the crippling condition of inaction the mind tends to pile up certainties in one direction in the form of over-simplified estimates of the characters of the two parties.

Even in sport a similar tendency is found. A supporter of Cambridge, looking at a photograph of the Oxford cricket eleven, is reported by C. E. Montague to have said: 'Look at them! The hangdog expressions! The narrow, ill-set Mongol eyes! The thin, cruel lips! Prejudice apart, would you like to meet that gang in a quiet place on a dark night?' Here no action is required except that of supporting whole-heartedly one's own side. Even that, however, can be done most comfortably by over-simplified judgements. It is easier to be whole-heartedly 'for' one side and 'against' the other if we attribute all the virtues to the one and all the vices to the other.

In history too we fall into this way of thinking. We make such a partition of the vices and the virtues, for example, between the Catholics and the Protestants in the history of religious wars and persecutions, between Reds and Whites in the Russian civil war, and even between Hurons and Mohicans when we read the Red Indian novels of Fenimore Cooper.

Education has, in the past, often fostered the tendency to acceptance of predigested thinking. Let us, for example, cast our minds back to the fragments of English history we retain from our school days. John and Richard III were 'bad' kings — not merely bad 'on the whole', but in all respects — oppressive, cruel, and tyrannical in their public lives and with no redeeming features in their home lives. Edward III and Henry V, on the other hand, were examples of 'good' kings. Perhaps we know now that competent historians do not endorse such drastic judgements and that the best modern history books for schools do not contain them. Our first reaction towards those who 'white-wash' Richard III is uncomfortable indignation. We feel that they are the sort of people who try to get notoriety by questioning what everyone knows to be true.

The same kind of thing happened in subjects other than history. We learned that Shakespeare was a great poet, and, if it was not taught, the over-simplified statement that all he wrote was perfect was at least implied. So the same shocked indignation has often greeted those who have tried intelligently to separate the fine grain from the chaff in Shakespeare's writing. Shakespeare was regarded as 'good' like Edward III and Henry V. Those who criticized him disturbed habitual predigested thinking.

In spite of all the hard things which may justly be said against predigested thinking, its service to action is of an importance not to be forgotten. Our enthusiasm for straight thinking must not blind us to the fact that what we do is more important than what we think. We must act effectively, even though we may be too clever to fall into the snares of predigested thinking. If we do not accept predigested thinking as a stimulus to effective action, we must learn to act effectively without it. So important is action that we can reasonably condemn as crooked thinking any device in thought which has as its purpose the evasion of useful or necessary action. 'There is much to be said on both sides, so I shall do nothing about it,' is a common type of thinking of those who are too intelligent to fall into the pitfall of popular predigested thinking, and it is itself a pitfall just as dangerous. Let us call it academic detachment from practical life.

There is, in politics, much to be said for Conservatism, much for Liberalism, and much for Socialism. But if we realize this so fully that we do not cast a vote at all, we are doing less than our neighbours who see less clearly than ourselves. Something is going to happen as a result of the poll, and the effect of our abstention from voting is as likely to affect the result in an undesirable way as any of the three possibilities of voting. By not voting we have not really escaped from the requirement of playing a part in the election; we have only made it impossible that our part will be a useful one.

We cannot escape the necessity for action, and our conviction that there is much to be said on all sides does not absolve us from the necessity for acting vigorously and effectively on the side on which we think the truest and wisest things can be said. If we are driving a motor vehicle across an open space and an obstacle appears in front of us, we can avoid it by going to the left or to the right. The arguments for both may be about equally balanced. We must, however, do either one or the other whole-heartedly without allowing the excellent case for the other side to affect our action. If we are content to say that there is much to be said in favour of both sides and drive straight on, we shall be in danger of breaking our necks.

The path of wisdom is to act in an effective and wholehearted manner on the side which seems to us, on the whole, to be the best. Realization of all that can be said on the other side should make us tolerant of those opposed to us and ready to revise our courses of action under the influence of new evidence, but it must not be allowed to interfere with the effectiveness of our action in the direction which we have calmly and clear-sightedly chosen. We must steer a middle course between the whirlpool of predigested thinking and the rock of academic detachment.

Although predigested thinking may have some practical usefulness, it is obviously a hindrance to straight thinking. If truth, and not idleness or convenience, is our aim, it is not to be tolerated. Even though predigested thinking is narrowly useful in providing motives for strenuous action, there is a wider sense in which its results are highly dangerous. Predigested thinking about our enemies while a war is on may help us to fight effectively, but it is also the continuance of that kind of thinking about the people of other nations which goes on between wars and during periods of international tensions that carries the seeds of future wars and may lead to inconceivable disasters. If the clear thinking which sees problems in their full complexity were to make us worse fighters and better keepers of the peace, the world as a whole would be the gainer.

A public man who shows by his speeches that he applies the over-simplifications of predigested thinking to international affairs (by, for example, referring to the Government of another nation as a 'group of murderers') should be deprived of his office and given an occupation in which this kind of thinking would be more useful. He might, for example, find a congenial field of usefulness as a cheer-leader in an American university football game. Predigested thinking in affairs inside the nation is no better. One cannot know how much strife and ineffectiveness in action may result from predigested thinking about relations between the sexes, about strikes and profit-making and about differences in skin-colour.

CHAPTER XIII

PITFALLS IN ANALOGY

IN THE course of explaining any rather abstract matter, it is an advantage to use a concrete illustration in order to make one's meaning clear. A psychologist, for example, trying to explain Freud's theory of the origins of neurotic disturbances from instinctive tendencies that have no useful outlet in behaviour, may compare this situation with steam coming out from leaks in the boiler of a steam-engine. Such illustrations are a common and useful device in explanation. A mental picture may be found easier to understand than an explanation in words.

The psychologist giving this illustration may be supposed to be merely intending to give a vivid picture of an abstract matter so that his hearers may be able to grasp the theory he is trying to explain; he does not intend his analogy to create in his hearers a conviction of the truth of that theory. When, on the other hand, a concrete illustration is used to create conviction of the truth of whatever it illustrates, or when it implies that truth in order to deduce some new conclusions, it is no longer a mere illustration; it is then an *argument from analogy*.

An example of an argument from analogy is to be found in a newspaper correspondence in which one writer suggested that the prosperity of the country might be restored by a revival of internal trade. An opponent derided this suggestion by saying that a dog could not live by eating its own tail. Let us consider this analogy carefully. If we assume the tail of an animal will go on growing after being bitten off (which is quite possible though not, as it happens, true of a dog), then the case of such an animal eating its own tail does present some analogy with a country living on internal trade. The body-building and energy-supplying elements in the food of the dog correspond to the consumable goods in the country. The argument is intended to prove that the country could not continue to exist without importation of such goods from outside.

On looking more deeply into the argument we see that there are vital differences between the two cases which vitiate the analogy. In the body of a dog there is necessary wastage of its food-stuffs to supply the animal with energy, and no possibility of replacement of this wastage except by taking in food from outside. It is physically impossible for the dog to generate his own proteins and carbohydrates from nothing; so, however generously his tail went on growing, he would be bound to die of starvation in the end if he had nothing but that to eat. The consumable goods of a country differ in this essential respect. Wealth can be generated in a country without taking in anything from outside, and this happens whenever labour is usefully employed. Every time a man sows a grain of corn and reaps an ear, or joins together two or more pieces of material to form a serviceable instrument, he is increasing the country's goods. The point, therefore, at which the dog eating his own tail supports the conclusion of the argument is the very respect in which the analogy is imperfect. What is contended may well be true, but it certainly cannot be proved by this argument.

I have also heard the democratic election of members of Parliament or of Congress attacked on the ground that children are not regarded as capable of electing their own teachers. Again, however, the analogy is obviously imperfect. Adult men and women are presumed to know more about the qualities required of an efficient ruler than children know about those of a good teacher. Moreover, governing and teaching are such very different functions that a method of selection serviceable in the one case may not be in the other. In addition, the democratic selection of the governing class partly serves to secure that those who rule shall not do so in their own interest; no similar problem is supposed to arise with teachers. In fact there is so little analogy between the selection of teachers and a Parliamentary election that no conclusions can safely be drawn by analogy from one to the other, whatever other weighty and reasonable objections may be urged against democracy.

The use of analogy in thought or communication is not necessarily wrong, although an argument based on analogy always needs critical examination. Analogy is the way in which much of our thinking is guided; when we meet an unfamiliar situation which we do not understand, we try to think of something familiar which resembles it and to use that as a guide to the new situation. What happens in the familiar case is what we expect to happen in the unfamiliar one, and very generally this expectation is fulfilled. So analogy proves itself a reasonably good guide to conduct; it becomes dangerous, however, when the conclusions to which it points are regarded as certain and not merely as probable.

Reduced to its bare bones, the argument from analogy has the form that because some thing or event N has the properties a and b which belong to M, it must have the property c which also belongs to M. Displayed like this, the argument does not sound a very convincing one.

Things which are alike in some respects differ in others. It may be that a and b are properties in which M and N resemble one another, while c may happen to be a property in which M differs from N. A whale resembles a fish in the general shape of its body and in the fact that it lives in water. If we knew no better, an argument from analogy would lead us erroneously to suppose that the whale also resembled a fish in breathing by gills instead of lungs. There is a well-known principle in arguing from analogy that we can only safely argue from the possession of one set of characters to another if there is a causal connection between them. Even this principle would not, however, save us from error here, because the possession of gills is causally connected with the fact of living in water. This just happens to be a character in which whales differ from fishes.

An argument by analogy is not always expanded into a clearly recognizable form. When a writer refers to 'the keen edge of a man's intellect' or to 'filling the mind of the child with facts', an analogy is implied, in the one case between an intellect and a knife or sword, in the other between a mind and a bucket, bag, or box. Such an analogy, implied by the choice of words but not definitely expressed, is a *metaphor*. A metaphor may be used merely for the purpose of illustration, but if (whether purposely or not) the user of a metaphor draws any new conclusions from the implied analogy, then he is using the argument from analogy although in a somewhat disguised form. If, for example, one said: 'The keen edge of the intellect will be blunted by frequent use', one would be using a metaphor as the basis for an argument by analogy. The argument would obviously be a weak one since the opposite conclusion would have been drawn if one had started with such an analogy as that of the intellect with the bodily muscles which become more efficient through frequent use and become atrophied if they are not used.

In the same way, one may hear the mind of a child compared with a container which may be filled with facts and ideas as a milk jug can be filled with milk. The implication of this comparison is that, like a milk jug, the mind has a limited capacity for facts and ideas and that when a certain number are acquired, there will be no room for more. This conclusion depends, however, on the arbitrary choice of an analogy. One might have thought of the child's mind as a kind of organization in which the more facts and ideas it contains, the more connections there will be for introducing new ones. That would be a different analogy which would lead to different practical consequences. The question as to which is the more appropriate analogy and which is the better guide to educational practice cannot be settled merely by examination of the analogies themselves; it must be discovered by research into the facts of the child's acquisition of knowledge. The original analogy is useful as a guide as to what we may look for in this research; the choice of analogies cannot be taken as a sure guide as to what we shall find in it.

That analogy can be a useful guide to thought is shown by the large part it has played in the development of science. Many of the conceptions that have guided scientific theory have been analogies from familiar objects. Thus atoms and electrons were thought of and treated as if they were tiny fragments of solid matter, and the aether of space as if it were an elastic fluid with peculiar properties. The success with which the science of physics used these conceptions to build up a consistent body of knowledge and to predict facts which turned out on investigation to be true led to a mistaken trust in the analogies which had been used. It led even to a forgetting of the fact that these mechanical principles were analogies and not direct descriptions of physical realities.

Yet a point was reached at which these analogies broke down. There were properties of electrons which were not conceivably those of lumps of matter however small, and it was found that if all space were filled with an aether, this substance must have the absurd property of both moving and being stationary with respect to the earth.

So physical theory has turned away from such concrete analogies and expressed its theories by means of mathematical equations. By doing this, it has become incomprehensible to most of us, for we feel that we can only comprehend what we can think of in terms drawn from what we can see and handle, that is by analogies with the outside world of reasonably large objects. Such analogies, however, do not help us to grasp a four-dimensional space-time system or to get hold of the ideas of quantum mechanics. We feel that we must think of atoms as tiny bits of matter or not think about them at all.

The fact that many of the analogies used in the early development of physics broke down in the end does not mean that the using of them was a mistake that held up the growth of true ideas in science. The physical analogies were, on the contrary, an important guide to the scientific thought of the time when they were in use. It was by the use of the analogies as guides to observation that it became clear in what respects they were inappropriate. It was only those who clung to the old analogies after they had been shown to be inappropriate who held up the growth of science. The analogies themselves were a means by which science advanced, but they were a means that had to be discarded when it was no longer useful.

The *caloric* theory of heat is a good example of a scientific analogy which was useful at the beginning for directing expectations but which had to be discarded when newly discovered facts showed it to be inappropriate. On this theory the heating of a body was explained on the analogy of adding one material body to another. It was supposed that a substance called 'caloric' was added to a body as it was heated and was removed from it as the body cooled. This is not the way we think about the matter now, but it is not to be regarded as a mere mistake. It was an explanation that advanced the understanding of heat a certain way. It would lead to the expectation that heating a body would increase its volume and its weight. The first of these expectations was (with a few exceptions) fulfilled; bodies do generally get larger as they are heated. They do not, however, increase in weight; if heating is the addition of caloric, then caloric must be without weight. The first striking fact that contradicted the expectations of the caloric theory was the observation that when metals are reduced to fine filings as in boring guns, a very large amount of heat is given out. A number of considerations render untenable the obvious explanation in terms of the caloric theory that caloric has been squeezed out of the metal by the process of boring. Here evidently a new way of thinking about the matter is demanded; the analogy of heat with a material substance had to be abandoned, and it was replaced by a new analogy in which heat was regarded as movement.

The case of the caloric theory illustrates the general principle that analogies may be a useful guide as to what facts to look for but they are never final evidence as to what the facts are. If one regards the correspondent who compared a country depending on internal trade with a dog eating its own tail as putting forward an analogy as a guide to what might be expected to be the case, this could be accepted as a useful first step in thinking about a controversial matter. The next step is to examine the analogy for its appropriateness. In this case the analogy is found to break down, and, like the caloric theory of heat, it must be discarded. But the realization of the inappropriateness is also a step towards understanding the matter under discussion. Someone else may think of a better analogy which may also be examined for its appropriateness. This is all part of a possible fruitful discussion which may lead to a better understanding of the matter discussed.

That the use of analogy is a possible manner of productive thinking is as suggested by its history. It was used as a main method of discussion by the wise men of ancient China. One of these (Hui Tzu) is reported on one occasion to have been told by his king to say things plainly and not to use analogies. He replied that this would be impossible since explaining is necessarily a process of making intelligible what is not known by comparing it with what is known.

An example of the old Chinese use of analogy is to be found in an argument between Mencius and Kao Tzu as to whether human nature is basically good or whether it is neither bad nor good. Kao Tzu said: 'Human nature does not show any preference for good or bad just as water does not show any preference for either east or west.' Mencius replied: 'It certainly is the case that water does not show any preference for either east or west, but does it show the same indifference to high and low? . . . There is no man who is not good; there is no water that does not flow downwards.'

Here it is to be noticed that the fact that a certain conclusion can be inferred from an analogy is not accepted as, in itself, a sufficient reason for accepting that conclusion as correct. Mencius points out that a slightly different analogy would lead to an altogether different conclusion. It is, in fact, necessary to examine the appropriateness of the analogy which has been used.

These are examples where analogy is serving a justifiable purpose. The use of analogy, however, becomes crooked argumentation when an analogy is used not as a guide to expectations but as a proof of a conclusion; not to see how well the analogy fits the facts but as in itself a proof that a certain conclusion is true. Let us call this an *argument by mere analogy*. If the correspondent who said that a dog cannot live by eating its own tail regarded this (as he probably did) as sufficient proof that a country cannot thrive by internal trade, he was guilty of arguing by mere analogy. Of course, the conclusion of such an argument may happen to be a true one because the expectation aroused by the analogy may happen to be fulfilled. It remains the case that the analogy is not sufficient proof of the conclusion.

Although it is apparent that an argument from mere analogy is not logically a sound ground for belief, it does seem to be a very effective way of inducing belief. This property of inducing belief is a concern of psychology rather than of logic. It seems to be the case that any analogy (good, imperfect, or obviously absurd) tends to produce conviction of the truth of what is asserted in the same immediate and unreasoning way as do repeated affirmation or a good slogan. If a speaker puts forward an argument in the form 'A is B, just as C is D' (where A and B are abstract or controversial while C and D are concrete and familiar), then his hearers will tend to believe that A is really B without considering how close is the analogy between A/B and C/D. If the relationship between C and D can be clearly pictured in the hearer's mind, this seems to make the process of conviction easier, although this may not be essential to it; the mere fact that the argument is in the form of an analogy is often enough to produce immediate acceptance.

If, for example, a lecturer on mental healing says that right thinking will remove disease from our bodies just as a policeman will remove a burglar, his audience may be more strongly convinced of the truth of his statement than they would have been by the mere assertion that right thinking will remove disease from our bodies without any supporting analogy. Here the analogy is a very imperfect one; the resemblance between right thinking removing disease and a policeman removing a burglar is not even close enough to create reasonable expectation, still less to constitute proof. An opponent might say that mere thinking can no more remove disease than can dreaming about a policeman remove a burglar. Although the analogy is imperfect, however, it may be effective in producing conviction simply because it is an analogy. The mental picture of a policeman removing a burglar may be sufficient to produce belief that right thinking will remove disease.

No doubt this power of analogy to produce conviction is the reason why at the time of elections, abstract thinking is very largely replaced by picturesque metaphors and analogies. Flowing tides, harpooned walruses, opponents trimming their sails or casting away their sheet anchors, replace the more prosaic ways of thinking in normal times. No doubt it all aids impassioned conviction, although it may be doubted whether this kind of thinking does much towards solving the real problems of the country.

Thus a Conservative speaker reproached the leader of the Liberal party with 'sailing as near to the Socialist wind as he can without upsetting his frail craft'.[1] This reference contains no ground beyond mere assertion for the suggestion that it was the policy of the Liberals to be as Socialistic as possible, but this assertion, being thrown into the form of a metaphor implying an analogy, is likely to carry more conviction than the bare verbal statement. The picture of the Liberal leader timorously edging his boat as close to the wind as he dare sticks in the mind persistently and is accepted readily; if the speaker had said bluntly what he meant instead of putting it in the form of an analogy, it is probable that his hearers would have been less inclined to believe him.

The tendency of a vivid metaphor or analogy to create conviction in the absence of rational grounds for that conviction makes possible a more extreme form of the crooked argument which we may call the *argument from forced analogy*. In this

[1] To object that sailing too near the wind is not liable to upset a boat, but only to make it stop, would be to lay oneself open to a just charge of 'diversion by irrelevant objection' (p 46). It shows, however, ignorance and incompetence to make such a slip in an analogy or in a metaphor, for, even if the objection is not made, it will occur to the minds of many hearers and interfere with the process of creating belief. Many parliamentary candidates in fishing constituencies have aroused mirth instead of conviction by inept metaphors of fishing and sailing. Of the same order of error is the 'mixed metaphor' in which different parts of the picture suggested are inconsistent with one another, such as a newspaper report during the first World War which referred to British soldiers 'opposed to a numerical superiority of the cream of the German Army tuned to concert pitch'.

more extreme case, the argument is thrown into the form of an analogy or metaphor when there is not sufficient resemblance between the things compared to form even a basis for expectation that they would resemble each other in the respect under discussion. A Victorian bishop said, for example, that virtue grows when watered by war's red rain. Judged rationally this is nonsense, however effective it may have been in convincing its audience that virtue was promoted by war. The bishop might as well have said that vice grows when watered by war's red rain, or that virtue withered when sprayed by war's red defoliant. Such an argument has so little logical justification that one must attribute its use to a recognition (perhaps unconscious) of the psychological fact that analogies tend to induce belief.

The argument from forced analogy differs only in degree from the argument from mere analogy, but it is convenient to treat them as two kinds of crooked thinking since they are liable to occur in different situations and they require different methods of refutation. Arguments from mere analogy commonly occur in serious discussions and are best dealt with by the method already employed of considering where the analogy breaks down. Forced analogies, on the other hand, are commonly found in public speeches. Their looseness is too obvious to stand against the kind of criticism they would meet in free discussion. They rely for their effect on the readiness of the mind to accept immediately any vivid metaphorical or analogical presentation of a matter. When one finds oneself driven to belief by a well-worded analogy like that of virtue watered by war's red rain, one can begin by examining how close the analogy is. Realizing that it is not at all close, one can try other analogies, as that of vice watered by war's red rain. Finding that these have no less force than the original analogy, the nature of the device used is apparent and its effect in forcing conviction disappears.

CHAPTER XIV

STRAIGHT THINKING

SO FAR we have been considering crooked thinking and dishonest argumentation. This leads to the question of what kind of thinking is sound and productive of real knowledge and of how communication can be used for the purpose of enlightenment rather than of persuasion. Our knowledge of the dishonest tricks of argument should not lead us to suppose that there is no profitable form of discussion; the purpose of charting the rocks is to know where the deep water lies, and knowledge of the dishonest methods of argument should help us to keep our own contributions to argumentation along profitable lines.

Nothing is a greater help to straightening our own thought than discussion with other people. But that discussion must be by methods very different from those of the propagandist who sets out to convince his opponent by fair means or foul, or of the debater who regards discussion as a kind of warfare in which the aim is victory over an opponent rather than the clearing of one's own mind as well as his.

One obvious condition that must be fulfilled before a real discussion can take place is that both parties must have a sufficiently lowly opinion of the finality of their own judgements to be willing to have their opinions changed by what the other person tells them. That is a condition which many people find rather difficult to attain, but, for those who do attain it, discussion with another person can result in a reasonably based change of opinion in either of two ways. First, his opponent may inform him of facts which he did not know before. Secondly, his opponent may point out inconsistencies between various opinions that he already holds.

A good example of opinions being modified by the kind of discussion in which those disputing are led to face the inconsistency between various opinions that they hold is provided by the dialogues of Socrates as reported by Plato. In these, the method of Socrates was to ask questions of the other person, very often getting him at first to pronounce a general opinion and then getting him to say what he thought on particular points arising from that general opinion. It then appeared that the person questioned did not agree with some of the implications of the general opinion he had first expressed and so he was invited to revise that general opinion until he had stated it in a way which led to no conclusions that he would not accept. For example, in the opening pages of *The Republic*, one of the companions of Socrates put forward an opinion on the nature of justice as 'giving every man his due'. By questioning the man who put forward this view, Socrates managed to convince him that this way of looking at justice implied other things which the man did not believe to be true, such as that justice was only useful to those who are at war or only useful for things that are not used, and also that the just man was a sort of thief. Since these seemed to be implied by the view that justice was giving every man his due, and since the man who had said that justice was giving every man his due did not believe these implications of his opinion about justice, he was led to conclude that he did not really believe that justice was giving every man his due.

He had thus been led to change his opinion as a result of discussion, by having been shown his opinion implied something that he thought was not true. Discussion has been of value to him in straightening out his thought by revealing inconsistencies which he had not suspected. This is an example of how discussion may help straight thinking when the discussion is honest and the people discussing are willing to change their minds. Indeed, an objection one can have to the Socratic dialogues as examples of straight discussion is that Plato makes it always appear that those who argued with Socrates were led to change their minds, while Socrates himself never seemed to do so.

It might be supposed that all that Socrates was doing might as well have been done by his companions themselves. He was revealing inconsistencies which were already present in their own thought; in other words, he was showing them what they really thought. If he was just doing that, it looks as if they might as well have done it for themselves. In a sense they might, but probably would not. We can all have many inconsistent opinions whose inconsistency we are not able to recognize until someone else shows it to us. I was once doing an experiment on a group of people to find the degree of self-consistency of their opinions. The amount of inconsistency revealed in their answers was surprising. For example, a large number both asserted that every statement in the Bible was literally true and also denied that Jonah emerged alive after having been swallowed by a great fish. It was not that they did not know that there was a statement in the Bible that Jonah was swallowed by a great fish and afterwards came out alive; it was merely that these were two opinions which they had formed separately without relating them to one another. Discussion with another person might have brought these two opinions in relationship to one another; it is less likely that they would have been brought into relationship by the person's own thinking since the realizing of the lack of consistency in one's own thought is a somewhat uncomfortable experience which the mind tries to avoid.

Such communication or thinking, producing rationally grounded changes in opinion, may be called 'productive'.

That an argument in the form of a syllogism can be genuinely productive is often hidden from students of logic by the trivial and absurd example of a typical syllogism that the text-books of logic have inherited from Aristotle:

> *All men are mortal,*
> *Socrates is a man,*
> *Therefore, Socrates is mortal.*

Aristotle was a great thinker, so one may charitably suppose that he made up this ridiculous example of an argument on the spur of the moment, realizing that he could substitute a better one tomorrow, and happily not realizing that this would be preserved to confuse students of logic for two thousand years. It is plainly non-productive; no one has ever said after he heard it: 'I see. Socrates will die too. I never realized that before.' No new information is generated by this pseudo-argument because no one could know that all men were mortal unless they already knew that Socrates was mortal.

There can, however, be thinking of the same general pattern which does really generate new knowledge. Wertheimer has pointed out a very elementary example. Suppose that I am going to vote in an election. There are four voting rooms and I do not know which of these I am supposed to use. I ask a policeman and he asks me my name. When I have told him, he says: 'Those whose names begin with T vote in room C.'

What has happened may be expressed in the form of a syllogism:

> *Those whose names begin with 'T' vote in room C.*
> *Thouless has a name beginning with 'T',*
> *Therefore, Thouless votes in room C.*

Unlike the Socrates argument, this one does really generate a new piece of knowledge. The conclusion was not previously known either to the policeman or to myself. He knew the first premiss; I knew the second. It was only when these two came together that the conclusion emerged. This is a very elementary example of productive thinking. More typically the form of a productive argument is that in which a general principle is put forward as the first premiss. This may be agreed to by both disputants. One of the disputants then puts forward a particular case of that general principle which leads to a conclusion unacceptable to the other.

Let us suppose, for example, that X is defending a pacifist position which Y does not accept. Neither X nor Y approve of murder and X has no difficulty in getting Y to accept the general principle that it is wrong to destroy human life. X makes this the first premiss of his argument. It differs from the first premiss in the Socrates argument in the fact that we all assent to general moral principles without considering all the particular cases to which they can be applied. Y may, for example, assent to the proposition that it is wrong to destroy human life because he finds the idea of taking life repulsive or because he accepts the authority of the Fifth Commandment, 'Thou shalt not kill'. X makes a new application of this agreed principle when he points out to Y that making war destroys human life which cannot be reasonably denied by Y. X then concludes that it is wrong to make war, which is a proposition previously denied by Y, but which he must admit necessarily follows from premisses that he has agreed to.

X's argument may be put in the form:

> *All destroying of human life is wrong,*
> *War is a destroying of human life,*
> *Therefore, war is wrong.*

This is a productive argument of sound logical form and its rational upshot for Y must be one of two things. First, he may change his mind about the conclusion, and now agree that war is wrong, perhaps saying that he never thought of the matter in that way before. Alternatively (and more probably) he will modify his acceptance of the first premiss and says that he does not really accept the proposition that all destroying of human life is wrong, but only the destroying of life under certain specified conditions, such as for one's private gain or for revenge, but that it is right when ordered by lawful authorities as in executions or in war. In either case, something has been accomplished by the argument, Y's opinions have been changed by it.

Whether it is by discussion with other people or by one's own deliberation that straight thinking is achieved, its purpose is to promote sensible action. We try to think straight in order that we may do the right things. The scientific control achieved in medicine, in engineering, and in all the practical affairs of life to which it has been applied is an outstanding example of how effective action may be promoted by straight thinking.

The scientific method of studying the facts and using words unemotionally and critically to help in understanding the facts proves its value by giving us certain knowledge and reliable methods of controlling our environment. The ideal of straight thinking must be the application of the scientific habit of thought to all our practical problems, and the replacement of blind forces controlling our destinies by our own intelligent and conscious control. In some fields we have already begun to apply this conscious control. The diseases which at one time were blind forces under which we bowed (as we now submit ourselves to earthquakes, thunderstorms, and trade depressions) have now begun to be brought under conscious control by the development of the science of medicine.

In other fields, no less important than bodily health, we seem content to remain at the mercy of blind forces. Until the end of the First World War we allowed wars to happen as we did thunderstorms, as if they were forces of nature over which man could have no control. It was not until the League of Nations was started after that war that we made a beginning at the attempt to control war. It was a beginning based on little exact knowledge of the causes of war or of the social and psychological conditions under which men of different nations with divergent aims could come to agreement, and it failed to prevent the Second World War. Our second attempt to achieve the same end by means of the United Nations Organization does not at present seem to be leading to any greater success. Although the intentions may be sound, there is neither the necessary scientific understanding of the processes of international rivalry nor the necessary willingness on the part of the nations involved to forgo so much of their sovereignty as would be necessary to make international co-operation possible. Before wars can be brought under scientific control we shall have to obtain more exact knowledge of their causes and of the ways in which groups of men of different cultures and with divergent interests can work together, and we shall have to be more ready to make the sacrifices of national self-feeling which are necessary in order that this knowledge may be applied effectively.

Most people agree now that it would be a good thing if we could apply scientific understanding and control to the problems of international rivalry; not so many believe in applying the same principles to the processes of production and distribution in their own country. Yet one cannot reasonably be satisfied with the situation in which the goods produced in a country may be given in extravagant abundance to a few, while there are others who receive such a small share of the country's wealth that they have little more than the food necessary to keep them alive and the shelter necessary to keep them from dying of exposure. A century ago these processes of production and distribution were left to the blind forces due to the interaction between individual merchants and buyers, of employers of labour and manual workers. There was little attempt at conscious control directed by scientific understanding. Now we have begun to regard these forces as things which can be understood and brought under control, although this attempt to understand and control has been resisted by those who preferred to regard poverty as the same kind of evil as a tidal wave about which we can do nothing, rather than as the same kind of evil as a pestilence which can be controlled by scientific means.

We do not yet single-mindedly adopt the scientific attitude either towards the problem of war or towards that of poverty. The man who brings a scientific attitude of mind to the analysis of a dispute between his own country and another may be labelled a 'traitor'. When we suggest that poverty is an evil whose causes must be discovered and, at all costs, removed, we are still sometimes told that the life of societies follows unchangeable economic laws with which it is dangerous to tamper.

It is, no doubt, true that the life of societies may be said to follow economic laws in the same sense as it may be said that a motor-car obeys mechanical laws and the human body obeys physiological laws. But we are not content to say that a motor-car must follow mechanical laws and then leave it to go where it likes. On the contrary, we move its steering-wheel and its throttle until we have produced conditions in which the mechanical laws it obeys will carry it the way we want to go. We do not consider it dangerous to interfere with the working of its laws; we avoid danger by understanding those laws. If we are nevertheless tempted to feel afraid of interfering with the conditions under which economic laws work, we may ask ourselves whether it is not more dangerous to leave them uncontrolled when we see the terrible effects in human misery which follow from their uncontrolled action.

There seems no sufficient reason why we should adopt towards these problems an attitude altogether different from the one we adopt towards illness. Scientific methods have slowly replaced other methods in the treatment of disease, and, as a result, disease has come largely under our control, and the amount of this control is all the time increasing. When we are ill, the doctor does not encourage us to hope that we shall muddle through. He looks for the cause of our condition – an infection, an injury, or a system of ideas in our own mind – and he tries to remove that cause. He does not doubt that in sickness as in health our bodies obey physiological laws. He is not, however, content simply to say that and do nothing about it. By medicine, by surgical operation, or by other treatment, he puts our bodies in conditions in which physiological laws will work for and not against our health.

Behind his work is that of a great army of research workers who have made his treatment of us possible. These have not attacked the abuses of microbes in emotionally coloured phrases; they have instead impartially studied their habits and conditions of life. They have shown no reverence for modes of treatment (like bleeding) which merely have the recommendation that they are old. They have boldly challenged every ancient habit of thought in the science of healing until it has proved itself to be of value.

Our own individual illnesses can be cured by scientific methods. The diseases of the great society to which we belong cannot be so healed until we accept for national and international affairs the same basic scientific principle that the way to get rid of an evil is to discover its cause by the methods of scientific research and then to destroy that evil by removing its causes.

Such international organizations as the United Nations and such gatherings as peace conferences to end particular wars do not have the characteristics that would be required for a scientific attempt to prevent or to cure war. A United Nations discussion or a peace conference may be conducted by politicians skilled in emotional oratory. This skill may be used effectively in denouncing the potential or actual enemy whose representatives use the same method in reply. This is a method calculated to heighten international tensions, not to relieve them. The task of relieving international tensions may be regarded as one of social psychotherapy. An individual psychotherapist tries to help his patient to understand and to control the sources of conflict within himself. In the same way, the organizations for peace should have the aim of uncovering causes of tension between nations and helping both sides to advance to mutual understanding and mutual good-will. The members of such an organization would, of course, need a kind of training altogether different from that of the present national representatives in the United Nations. They would be trained as research scientists in social psychotherapy, not as politicians and orators. Their aim would be the relief of tensions between nations, not the promotion of the ends of their own nation.

This is a dream for the future; in the meantime our international affairs are analogous to the situation of travellers on a motor-car travelling at speed over an unmapped plain. The driver has not his hands on the wheel, for he knows neither where he wants to go nor how to get there if he did. When we suggest he should put his hands on the wheel and exercise his intelligence in thinking where he wants to go and how to get there, he turns to us with an idiotic smile and says that the car must obey mechanical laws and that we must trust our instinct for 'muddling through'. We know that the plain through which we are travelling has ravines and morasses in which lie the wrecked remains of cars which have travelled blindly across it in times long past. We know too that the advances of the technology of destruction are such that the effects of future accidents will be far more disastrous than were those of the past. Occasionally we do come into collision with other cars, but such collisions fill the survivors with such exalted emotions and are believed to be productive of such extraordinary virtues that no one blames the driver for the deaths of some of the passengers and the grave injuries to the car.

Occasionally the passengers are allowed to decide who shall have the privilege of sitting at the steering-wheel, but as they too do not believe in intelligent choice of route and know even less than the driver how to get there, and since the new driver may also sit with his hands off the wheel, these occasional lapses into apparently democratic control of the car have little practical importance.

We are now, however, beginning to realize that a car can only be driven in safety by conscious and intelligent control, that experience of car driving has shown that there is no such thing as an instinct for muddling through, that the relaxation of intelligent control means inevitable disaster, and that a car whose course is determined by merely mechanical laws is headed for a crash.

No one can know what is going to happen to that car in which we are all travelling. Our best chance of survival lies in applying to national and international affairs intelligent thought and conscious control. Our best chance of solving such problems as war, poverty, over-population, and pollution is to approach them in the same scientific spirit as we have now learned to apply to disease, sure that every effect has causes, that impartial scientific investigation will reveal those causes, and that intelligently guided effort can remove them.

The forces of irrationality are certainly strong and there is a great deal of power behind the crooked thinking that leads to readiness for war and hostility between people of different skin colour or of different religions. How can we effectively oppose these forces? They are indeed strong and attempts to promote dispassionate reasonableness seem to be weak against them. But a sufficiently persistent attitude of dispassionate reasonableness, adopted by enough people of all countries, skin-colours and religions may, in the end, wear down the strength of irrationality. We may be encouraged to notice that such dictators as Hitler, who have built their power on irrationality, have been afraid of the force of reasonableness. While Hitler's invective was bitter against the Jews and the Communists whom he regarded as active enemies, it was no less fierce against the Germans who tried to think objectively about social and international problems whom he called the 'liberals'. He may have been right in seeing in the development of dispassionate reasonableness at least as great a threat to power based on irrationality as that of violent opposition to such power.

An efficient democracy would be one based on such dispassionate reasonableness. Its members would be educated to distrust emotional language and the rest of the stock in trade of the exploiters of crooked thinking. They would have no reverence for old institutions or for old ways of thinking when these had outlived their usefulness. Such a democracy, informed and guided by scientific knowledge, could take conscious control of our social development and could reasonably hope to destroy those evils that now seem invincible. That would be a beneficent revolution which might take place if sufficient numbers of people wanted it badly enough. But the revolution must start with a change in our thinking.

THIRTY-EIGHT DISHONEST TRICKS WHICH ARE COMMONLY USED IN ARGUMENT, WITH THE METHODS OF OVERCOMING THEM

IN MOST textbooks of logic there is to be found a list of 'fallacies', classified in accordance with the logical principles they violate. Such collections are interesting and important, and it is to be hoped that any readers who wish to go more deeply into the principles of logical thought will turn to these works. The present list is, however, something quite different. Its aim is practical and not theoretical. It is intended to be a list which can be conveniently used for detecting dishonest modes of thought which we shall actually meet in arguments and speeches. Sometimes more than one of the tricks mentioned would be classified by the logician under one heading, some he would omit altogether, while others that he would put in are not to be found here. Practical convenience and practical importance are the criteria I have used in this list.

If we have a plague of flies in the house we buy fly-papers and not a treatise on the zoological classification of *Musca domestica*. This implies no sort of disrespect for zoologists, or for the value of their work as a first step in the effective control of flies. The present book bears to the treatises of logicians the relationship of fly-paper to zoological classifications.

Other books have been concerned with the appraisal of the whole of an argumentative passage without such analysis into sound and unsound parts as I have attempted. Undoubtedly it is also important to be able to say of an argued case whether it has or has not been established by the arguments brought forward. Mere detection of crooked elements in the argument is not sufficient to settle this question since a good argumentative case may be disfigured by crooked arguments. The study of crooked thinking is, however, an essential preliminary to this problem of judging the soundness of an argued case. It is only when we have cleared away the emotional thinking, the selected instances, the inappropriate analogies, etc, that we can see clearly the underlying case and make a sound judgement as to whether it is right or wrong.

The thirty-eight dishonest tricks of argument described in the present book are the following:

(1) *The use of emotionally toned words* (pp 10–25).
Dealt with by translating the statement into words emotionally neutral.

(2) *Making a statement in which 'all' is implied but 'some' is true* (pp 27–38).
Dealt with by putting the word 'all' into the statement and showing that it is then false.

(3) *Proof by selected instances* (pp 32–7).
Dealt with dishonestly by selecting instances opposing your opponent's contention or honestly by pointing out the true form of the proof (as a statistical problem in association) and either supplying the required numerical facts or pointing out that your opponent has not got them.

(4) *Extension of an opponent's proposition by contradiction or by misrepresentation of it* (pp 39–43).
Dealt with by stating again the more moderate position which is being defended.

(5) *Evasion of a sound refutation of an argument by the use of a sophistical formula* (pp 41–4).
Dealt with by analysis of the formula and demonstration of its unsoundness.

(6) *Diversion to another question, to a side issue, or by irrelevant objection* (pp 44–8).

Dealt with by refusing to be diverted from the original question, but stating again the real question at issue.

(7) *Proof by inconsequent argument* (pp 49–50).

Dealt with by asking that the connection between the proposition and the alleged proof may be explained, even though the request for explanation may be attributed to ignorance or lack of logical insight on the part of the person making it.

(8) *The argument that we should not make efforts against X which is admittedly evil because there is a worse evil Y against which our efforts should be directed* (pp 50–52).

Dealt with by pointing out that this is a reason for making efforts to abolish Y, but no reason for not also making efforts to get rid of X.

(9) *The recommendation of a position because it is a mean between two extremes* (pp 52–4).

Dealt with by denying the usefulness of the principle as a method of discovering the truth. In practice, this can most easily be done by showing that our own view also can be represented as a mean between two extremes.

(10) *Pointing out the logical correctness of the form of an argument whose premises contain doubtful or untrue statements of fact* (p 58).

Dealt with by refusing to discuss the logic of the argument but pointing out the defects of its presentations of alleged fact.

(11) *The use of an argument of logically unsound form* (pp 58–64).

Since the unsoundness of such arguments can be easily seen when the form of the argument is clearly displayed, an opponent who does this can be dealt with by making such a simple statement of his argument that its unsoundness is apparent. For one's own satisfaction when reading an argument of doubtful soundness, it will often be found useful to make a diagram.

(12) *Argument in a circle* (p 64).

(13) *Begging the question* (pp 65–6).

Both 12 and 13 can be dealt with in the same way as 11; by restating your opponent's argument in such a simple way that the nature of the device used must be clear to anyone.

(14) *Discussing a verbal proposition as if it were a factual one, or failing to disentangle the verbal and factual elements in a proposition that is partly both* (pp 67–77).

This is really an incompetent rather than a dishonest way of arguing. The remedy is to point out how much of the question at issue is a difference in the use of words and how much (if at all) it is a difference as to fact or values.

(15) *Putting forward a tautology (such as that too much of the thing attacked is bad) as if it were a factual judgement* (pp 71–72).

Dealt with by pointing out that the statement is necessarily true from its verbal form.

(16) *The use of a speculative argument* (pp 78–83).

Rebutted by pointing out that what is cannot be inferred from what ought to be or from what the speaker feels must be.

(17) *Change in the meaning of a term during the course of an argument* (pp 88–94).

Dealt with by getting the term defined or by substituting an equivalent form of words at one of the points where the term in question is used and seeing whether the use of this form of words will make true the other statement in which this term is used.

(18) *The use of a dilemma which ignores a continuous series of possibilities between the two extremes presented* (pp 103–5).

Dealt with by refusing to accept either alternative, but pointing to the fact of the continuity which the person using the argument has ignored. Since this is likely to appear over-subtle to an opponent using the argument, it may be strengthened by pointing out that the argument is the same as that of saying, 'Is this paper black or white?' when it is, in fact, a shade of grey.

(19) *The use of the fact of continuity between them to throw doubt on a real difference between two things (the 'argument of the beard') (pp 105–8).*

Dealt with by pointing out that the difference is nevertheless real. This again may be made stronger by pointing out that application of the same method of argument would deny the difference between 'black' and 'white' or between 'hot' and 'cold'.

(20) *Illegitimate use of or demand for definition (p 109).*

If an opponent uses definitions to produce clear-cut conceptions for facts which are not clear-cut, it is necessary to point out to him how much more complicated facts are in reality than in his thought. If he tries to drive you to define for the same purpose, the remedy is to refuse formal definition but to adopt some other method of making your meaning clear.

(21) *Suggestion by repeated affirmation (pp 111–14).*

(22) *Suggestion by use of a confident manner (pp 114–15).*

(23) *Suggestion by prestige (pp 115–18).*

The best safeguard against all three of these tricks of suggestion is a theoretical knowledge of suggestion, so that their use may be detected. All three devices lose much of their effect if the audience see how the effect is being obtained, so merely pointing out the fact that the speaker is trying to create conviction by repeated assertion in a confident manner may be enough to make this device ineffective. Ridicule is also often used to undermine the confident manner, or any kind of criticism which makes the speaker begin to grow angry or plaintive.

(24) *Prestige by false credentials (pp 115–18).*

The obvious remedy for this is, when practicable, to expose

the falsity of the titles, degrees, etc, that are used. The prestige then collapses.

(25) *Prestige by the use of pseudo-technical jargon* (pp 116–18)

Best dealt with by asking in a modest manner that the speaker should explain himself more simply.

(26) *Affectation of failure to understand backed by prestige* (pp 118–19).

Dealt with by more than ample explanation.

(27) *The use of questions drawing out damaging admissions* (pp 119–20).

Dealt with by refusal to make the admissions. The difficulty of this refusal must be overcome by any device reducing one's suggestibility to the questioner.

(28) *The appeal to mere authority* (pp 122–5).

Dealt with by considering whether the person supposed to have authority had a sound reason for making the assertion which is attributed to him.

(29) *Overcoming resistance to a doubtful proposition by a preliminary statement of a few easily accepted ones* (pp 128–30).

Knowledge of this trick and preparedness for it are the best safeguard against its effects.

(30) *Statement of a doubtful proposition in such a way that it fits in with the thought-habits or the prejudices of the hearer* (pp 133–5 and p 157).

A habit of questioning what appears obvious is the best safeguard against this trick. A particular device of value against it is to restate a questionable proposition in a new context in which one's thought-habits do not lead to its acceptance.

(31) *The use of generally accepted formulae of predigested thought as premises in argument* (pp 161–6).

The best way of dealing with predigested thinking in argument is to point out good-humouredly and with a backing of real evidence that matters are more complicated than your opponent supposes.

(32) *'There is much to be said on both sides, so no decision can be made either way'*, or any other formula leading to the attitude of academic detachment (pp 166–7).

Dealt with by pointing out that taking no action has practical consequences no less real than those which result from acting on either of the propositions in dispute, and that this is no more likely than any other to be the right solution of the difficulty.

(33) *Argument by mere analogy* (pp 169–78).

Dealt with by examining the alleged analogy in detail and pointing out where it breaks down.

(34) *Argument by forced analogy* (pp 178–9).

The absurdity of a forced analogy can best be exposed by showing how many other analogies supporting different conclusions might have been used.

(35) *Angering an opponent in order that he may argue badly* (pp 146–7).

Dealt with by refusing to get angry however annoying our opponent may be.

(36) *Special pleading* (pp 154–6).

Dealt with by applying one's opponent's special arguments to other propositions which he is unwilling to admit.

(37) *Commending or condemning a proposition because of its practical consequences to the hearer* (pp 157–8).

We can only become immune to the effect of this kind of appeal if we have formed a habit of recognizing our own tendencies to be guided by our prejudices and by our own self-interest, and of distrusting our judgement on questions in which we are practically concerned.

(38) *Argument by attributing prejudices or motives to one's opponent* (p 159).

Best dealt with by pointing out that other prejudices may

equally well determine the opposite view, and that, in any case, the question of why a person holds an opinion is an entirely different question from that of whether the opinion is or is not true.

A DISCUSSION ILLUSTRATING
CROOKED THINKING

IN ORDER to illustrate the foregoing list of dishonest arguments I have devised an imaginary conversation between three gentlemen in which as many dishonest devices as possible are used. The three disputants are supposed to be of reasonably good intelligence and intellectual honesty and to be using the devices without any conscious intention of scoring an unfair victory. The arguments have been chosen to illustrate crooked thinking, so that the whole conversation is worse than an average sample of intellectual after-dinner discussion. Most of the arguments, however, are identical with or similar in form to ones that I have heard used by quite intelligent people. I do not think that any part of the conversation is more crooked and unsound than can be heard at any place where intellectual conversation is carried on, although I admit that it would be difficult to find, in practice, a conversation in which there is so sustained a failure to argue straight on any problem. To that extent the conversation is a caricature, but a caricature made up of natural fragments.

I suggest that, at a first reading, readers should cover up my notes on the conversation, and write down all the pieces of crooked argumentation or thought that they can detect in the passage, referring when possible to numbers in the list of dishonest tricks in Appendix I. Afterwards they may wish to compare the fallacies they have detected with those pointed out in my notes. My notes do not claim to be either exhaustive or unprejudiced, and many readers will no doubt make a different list which has the same claim to be considered right as my own.

Those taking part in the conversation are B— a business man, P— a professor, and C— a clergyman. They are sitting over their port after dinner at B—'s home. The conversation is opened by the professor.

P.   I wonder what the result of the election will be.

B.   I trust the country will have the sense to return a sound and sensible business Government. What the country needs is a period of tranquillity, so that it can get back to prosperity.[1]

Another glass of port, Professor. C—, you know, calls himself a Socialist,[2] but I trust you will vote Conservative.

P.   As a scientist, I find myself in disagreement with all political parties. All seem to me to be equally unscientific. The vital problems of finding outlets for our expanding population and of weeding out the unfit can only be solved by the application of the scientific method to political problems. At present, I see no signs of any of the political parties realizing this, so I shall refrain from using my vote.[3]

---

[1] B— makes free use of emotionally toned words (No 1). 'Sound' and 'sensible' have more of emotional meaning than of any other. A Government which appears 'sound and sensible' to its supporters will be called 'conventional and uninspired' by its opponents. Similarly, 'tranquillity' has the same objective meaning as 'stagnation', but an opposite emotional meaning.

[2] B— here uses a phrase with a somewhat unfavourable emotional implication (No 1). It suggests some insincerity in C—'s Socialism.

[3] This is an example of an intellectual justification of academic detachment from practical life (No 32). P— is probably a man of higher intellectual ability than either of the others, but the practical outcome of his intellectual powers, so far as they affect the election, is the same as would result from his being too imbecile to find his way to the polling booth. His academic detachment is also shown by the two 'vital

C. No, no more port for me, thank you.

As a minister of the Gospel,[1] it seems to me that the great problem before us is the uplifting of the labouring masses.[2] I put my trust in an enlightened and Christianized Socialism.[3] I realize very well that our Labour Party is not ideal, but purified from its materialism . . .

B. [interrupting]. But what you don't realize, my dear fellow, is that its aims are materialist through and through.[4] Fill the worker's belly[5] and never mind his soul. That's not Christianity. There would be no room for parsons in the Socialist State.[6]

P. I have no objection to filling a man's belly. Our own are full, and we are the better for it.[7] I should fill every

---

problems' he mentions; they do not include the problem of securing that people have enough to eat.

Notice too that he begins by appealing to his prestige as a scientist (No 23).

[1] He too begins by appealing to his prestige (No 23).

[2] Here we first see one of the most striking features of the whole speech – its extreme vagueness. 'Uplifting' is a word used without any very precise meaning; so also is 'materialism'.

[3] Begging the question by the use of the emotionally toned word 'enlightened' (No 13). B— would not regard any Socialism as enlightened.

[4] The word 'materialist' as used by C— has, as we have seen, no exact meaning. But C— has made it clear that he has thought habits in connection with it, so B— takes advantage of those thought habits to advance his own view (No 30).

[5] B— might well be charged with special pleading (No 36) in this part of the second sentence. He has just been very much occupied with the business of filling his own belly without feeling that it was a reprehensible aim.

'Filling the belly' is a phrase with strong emotional meaning of disapprobation (No 1). The emotionally neutral phrase would be 'give the worker enough to eat'.

[6] Appealing to the practical interests of C— (No 37).

[7] P— deals with B—'s special pleading in the way recommended in

worker's belly, but stop this socialistic[1] business of robbing the industrious in order to support the idle and inefficient.[2] That is unbiological.[3]

B.   And the workers themselves will be the first to suffer when the country is ruined; look at the level of income-tax now.[4] It was private enterprise that built up the industrial system that gave us our prosperity.[5] That's what we must get back to if we want the country to prosper again.

C.   [slowly and impressively]. No man should be content

Appendix I – by applying the same words to other circumstances in which B— would not maintain his attitude of disapproval. He does not destroy the effect of B—'s emotional term 'filling the belly' by translating it into an emotionally neutral phrase, but robs it of its emotional implications just as effectively by applying it to their own dining.

[1] The termination '-ic' gives this word an emotional tone of disapproval (No 1). C— would have said 'socialist'. With the same effect one can say 'capitalistic', 'atheistic', 'militaristic', etc.

[2] Any judgement as to whether this is or is not a bad thing is made difficult by the use of emotionally toned words which predispose the hearer to think that it must be bad (No 1). The remark could be paraphrased in emotionally neutral language as 'taxing the rich in order to support the poor'. Put like this, it is clear that this is not self-evidently a wrong policy; it is then expressed in a way that leaves the hearers free to make a sensible judgement as to whether they think it right or wrong.

[3] This word 'unbiological' does not seem to do more than produce a feeling by its emotional tone of disapproval. The fact that it is a scientific word as well as an emotionally toned one lends it a spurious prestige which has no doubt a suggestive effect (No 25).

[4] His hearers might reasonably wonder whether B—'s dislike of a high income-tax was more the result of his anxiety lest the workers should be ruined than of his anxiety lest he himself might be ruined. The objection sounds better if it is not presented as a matter that affects his own interests.

[5] This is a typical product of predigested thinking (No 31). It is an over-simplified statement of a complex situation. The rise of industrialism brought prosperity to some individuals but also much misery and hardship to others.

with our industrialism while one child living under that system is short of food.[1]

B.   My dear C—, no one wants children to starve. Industrialism does more towards feeding children than all the socialistic theories in the world.[2] How many children does the Labour Party feed?[3]

C.   I hold no brief for any particular political party,[4] but I expect the Labour Party does as much or as little in direct relief of poverty as any other political party.[5]

[1] Whatever we may think of the matter of this remark, we must notice that the manner of its delivery is that of suggestion by the use of a confident manner (No 22). Also we may ask why children are brought into the argument. Middle-aged people can also be short of food. It may truly be argued that under-nutrition has worse effects on children than on those in later life, but that is not why C— mentioned children. He is taking advantage of emotional habits of thought in connection with children (No 30). In the same way a believer in non-resistance to evil is asked: 'Wouldn't you consider it right to use force to protect a helpless little child who was being maltreated by a powerful and brutal man?' He is never asked the equally reasonable question: 'Wouldn't you consider it right to use force to protect a helpless middle-aged stockbroker who was being maltreated by a powerful and brutal man?

[2] This argument depends on an ambiguity in the use of the word 'industrialism' (No 17). B— appears to be using it as equivalent to 'industry,' while C— used it for the particular conditions under which industry functions at the present time. The feeding of children would certainly not go on without 'industry' in the general sense, but it is not, therefore, dependent on any particular conditions under which industry functions.

[3] A diversion (No 6). This is also an example of special pleading (No 36), for no political party feeds children.

[4] Instead of challenging B—'s statement that industrialism feeds children, C— follows the diversion, and takes refuge in a characteristic vagueness. When defending Socialism, he does not mean any particular Socialist organization. If he were pressed by B—, it would probably become clear that he is similarly not prepared to defend any particular Socialist proposal.

[5] Not content with the evasion by vagueness, he successfully meets his opponent's special pleading in the standard manner.

P. Let us return to a point in the argument which interests me more than the merits or demerits of the Labour Party. You both seem to agree that children ought not to be starving. As a scientist,[1] I cannot agree with you. Nature effects all improvements in the race by a process of elimination of the unfit by natural selection. By natural selection, the horse has become strong and the greyhound swift. Starvation is one of Nature's weapons for eliminating the unfit.[2] The sight of her methods may offend our humaner feelings, but the attempt of sentimental philanthropy to interfere with them can only lead to degeneration of the human race.[3] A State-subsidized national health service which keeps alive the children of the unfit and the provision of free milk in schools are biological crimes.

C. [after a pause]. Is the swiftness of the greyhound the result of natural selection?[4] You surprise me, Professor; I thought that it was the result of breeding.[5]

[1] Again he appeals to prestige authority (No 23). Much of what he is about to say would hardly pass muster without some such support.

[2] The preceding three sentences are ordinarily accepted commonplaces of evolutionary biology. Their function in the argument is that of the few easily accepted propositions which overcome the resistance to a highly questionable one which follows (No 29). They are not, as may be supposed at first sight, logical steps leading up to the conclusion, for the conclusion to which they should lead is not that the intensive starvation of poor children should go on unchecked (which is the proposition that P— is defending), but that all children should be starved sufficiently to cause the death of the physically unfit. The statement about the horse and the greyhound is also an inappropriate analogy (No 33).

[3] P— uses very improperly the emotionally toned word 'sentimental' (No 1). If a given kind of philanthropy leads to degeneration of the human race, then that kind of philanthropy can fairly be called 'sentimental,' but not otherwise. The word should not be used in the course of an argument intended to prove that such philanthropy leads to racial degeneration.

[4] C— attempts a diversion by irrelevant objection (No 6).

[5] The sarcastic form of this remark is calculated to anger P— (No 35).

P.   Say the wolf, then. The argument remains the same.[1]
I want to see a race that has the biological virtues of strength,
fitness, and independence.

C.   I suppose the tape-worm and the liver-fluke became
parasitic by natural selection?[2]

P.   Yes, if you like.[3] Man is not a tape-worm or a liver-
fluke.[4]

C.   By what right do you call the children of the poor 'the
unfit'?[5] As a minister of the Gospel,[6] I protest against any such
statement. In the homes of the poor in my parish I find a level
of spiritual attainment far higher than is to be found amongst
the rich.[7]

---

[1] P— refuses to accept C—'s diversion or to become angry. It was,
of course, his blunder that made the irrelevant objection possible.

[2] Showing the imperfection of P—'s analogy of the effect of natural
selection on the horse, etc, by the expedient of suggesting that the same
analogy with different terms would point to an opposite conclusion.

[3] A form of words unfairly suggesting the unimportance of C—'s
objection.

[4] Meaning, of course, that man does not resemble these creatures
sufficiently for the purpose of analogy – a dishonest evasion of C—'s
point that the results of natural selection are not always desirable. P—
is saying in effect: 'Your analogy is imperfect', as if C— were bringing
forward a new argument by analogy of his own, whereas he is really
pointing to an imperfection in P—'s previous argument by analogy.
This is an example of an inconsequent argument (No 7), since it does
not really meet C—'s point, but only appears to do so.

[5] Here C— puts his finger on the worst weakness of P—'s argument.
That those who, through poverty, are most likely to suffer from hunger
in a competitive-individualist pattern of society are also those who are
'unfit' in the biological sense, is an unproved assumption which only
needs dragging into the limelight to be disposed of. It is essential to
P—'s argument, for without it the abolition of the philanthropy he
condemns would not lead to a process of natural selection.

[6] C— has made a perfectly good point and has no need to support it
with prestige suggestion (No 23).

[7] Still less should he support it by an extreme statement which, if true,
would be inconsequent (No 7), but which is no more likely to be true

P.   I am not a minister of the Gospel but a mere scientist, and I must confess that I have no very clear idea as to what is meant by a 'level of spiritual attainment'.[1] So far as my in-expert observations go, I have not noticed the superiority you refer to.[2]

As to the relationship between poverty and unfitness, I regard poverty itself as a mark of biological unfitness. It is a failure of social adaptation. The socially maladapted are the biologically unfit. The poor are those who have been unable to adapt themselves to the condition of the society in which they live. They are biologically unfit because they are socially maladapted.[3]

C.   My training has been in philosophy rather than science, and I fear I am unable to carry on a discussion in the bar-barous jargon of the modern scientist.[4] Perhaps you would be good enough to define this term 'social maladaptation'.[5]

---

than its opposite, and is open to the objection that 'spiritual attainment' is something too vague to be made the subject of a quantitative state-ment. C— has, in fact, made a diversion very unfavourable to himself.

[1] This is the trick of affectation of ignorance backed by prestige (No 26). The word 'mere' is ironical and must not blind us to the fact that P— is again calling attention to his prestige as scientist. He is saying in effect: 'I am a learned man but I cannot understand you; you must be talking nonsense.'

[2] Not content with this, he also denies C—'s alleged fact. For the moment he accepts C—'s diversion, since it gives him the opportunity of scoring a cheap victory.

[3] The substitution of 'social maladaptation' for 'unfitness' makes his remarks sound more scientific, but it does not really get over the diffi-culty. He is relying on the prestige effect of technical jargon (No 25). Realizing the weakness of this substitution, he uses another trick – repeated affirmation (No 21). He says it four times.

[4] In a slightly different form, this is essentially the same trick of affecting ignorance (No 26) as was used by P—.

[5] If C— means to press for a formally correct definition (as he prob-ably does), this is an example of an unfair badgering to define (No 20).

B.   But seriously, Professor.[1] Do you mean that biology would have us let the poor and their families starve?

P.   I do not say that our superfluous population should be allowed to starve.[2] The remedy which biology suggests is that they should never be allowed to be born.

B.   But here they are; they have been born.[3] What are we to do about it if we don't feed them? What's your solution?

P.   Effective control of our birth-rate from the lower strata of society is the only possible solution. Then there would be no surplus population to bother about.[4] At present we are breeding from the dregs of the nation. The degraded and criminal elements in our population are increasing at an enor-

---

P— could fairly be asked to explain what he means, but is unlikely to be able to provide a formally correct definition on the spur of the moment. If he could, it would give the idea more precision and rigidity than the facts it is trying to describe, for in fact social maladaptation is a phenomenon showing continuous variation. We are all more or less imperfectly fitted to our social environments, and there is no sharp point at which this imperfection becomes so great as to amount to social maladaptation.

[1] Fortunately B— intervenes and prevents the discussion from being diverted to a somewhat personal squabble about science and philosophy. His first words are a mere verbal habit with hardly any meaning. He does not suppose that P— and C— have been joking.

[2] Actually, this is precisely what he did say; he is now making a diversion (No 6) to a much more defensible position. He is using the trick of first stating an extreme position and then making a diversion to a more moderate one. P— covers the diversion by simply denying what he previously said. He is no longer defending the unchecked operation of natural selection but the attempt to achieve its ends by other less painful methods. A very considerable shifting of the ground of debate!

[3] B— attempts to check the diversion and to go on discussing the same problem.

[4] P— gives further evidence of his academic detachment from practical affairs. He refuses to consider the practical problem which is worrying B—, which, however, would still exist for twenty years or so even if P—'s solution were put into practice immediately and proved effective.

mous rate, while the birth-rate of the intelligent and industrious is falling.[1] I see nothing but disaster in front of our race
if this process is allowed to go on unchecked.

C. And you propose to stop this by interference with the
natural rate of reproduction?

P. How else?

C. It would be an outrage to human dignity to apply the
methods of the stud farm to the sacred function of human
parenthood.[2] I cannot discuss such a subject.[3] It is a proposal
that is offensive to every enlightened conscience.[4]

P. Why?

C. Because it is opposed to natural morality. It is an
interference with Nature.[5] Man would not have been given an

---

[1] P—'s rapid shifts from 'the poor' to 'the socially maladapted' to
'the dregs of the nation,' and finally to 'the degraded and criminal
elements in the population', with no indication that he realizes he is
changing the subject of discussion, shows a background of predigested
thinking (Chapter XI). All of these different groupings of men are fused
under a single general idea with all the very important differences left
out. Also we notice another diversion (No 6). He started by talking
about that part of the population which needs social assistance, but goes
on to discuss the different problem of the relatively lower birth-rate of
the middle classes (who are meant to be indicated by the term 'intelligent and industrious'). This is clearly a different problem.

[2] An argument which depends entirely on emotionally toned words
(No 1).

[3] This is obvious. If C— could transcend the limitations of his
thought-habits (Chapter X) sufficiently to consider P—'s proposition
as a possibility, he would be able to attack it more effectively.

[4] Begging the question by the use of an emotionally toned word (No
13). He means by an 'enlightened' conscience one to which the proposal
was offensive. P—, on the other hand, would regard a conscience as
enlightened if the proposal were acceptable to it.

[5] Special pleading (No 36), because C— would not accept the general
proposition that any interference with Nature was wrong, and has given
no further objection to this particular interference with Nature which
would make it wrong while others were right.

instinct to reproduce his kind if he had been intended to inter-fere with the results of that instinct.[1]

P.   Aren't tilling the ground and giving medicine to the sick interferences with Nature?[2] You give free milk to the illegitimate child of criminal parents, and then, when he follows the only course of behaviour possible to anyone with his heredity,[3] you interfere with Nature by locking him up. Wouldn't it have been better to have interfered with Nature earlier on and sterilized his father? Remember that if you had started with his chromosomes you would have been just as bad a criminal.

C.   I cannot accept such an account of human nature. It undermines the foundations of morality.[4] Either every man is a free agent and accountable for all his actions to the God who made him, or else he is the helpless victim of his heredity and there is no goodness or heroism in the world.[5] As a Christian philosopher,[6] I accept the first of these alternatives.

---

[1] A speculative argument (No 16). C— is arguing not from what is but from what must be. Also another bad specimen of special pleading; C— would certainly not believe that a man must never interfere with what results from his instincts.

[2] P— deals with C—'s special pleading in the manner recommended in Appendix I.

[3] Here, and again in the last sentence, P— puts forward an extreme statement where a moderate one is true (No 2). He says in effect: 'All persons with criminal heredity become criminals', whereas the only justifiable statement is that there is a tendency for persons with criminal heredity to become criminals.

[4] Condemning the proposition as untrue, not because the evidence is against it but because of its practical consequences (No 37).

[5] Presenting two extreme alternatives, whereas in fact there are an infinite number of possibilities lying in between these two extremes (No 18). Most sensible people would, I think, accept one of the intermediate positions.

[6] Again appealing to his prestige. In point of fact, C—'s grounds for

P. Well, what would you do with the child with a criminal heredity? Are you in favour of rearing him at public expense and imprisoning him when he grows up?[1]

C. I should remove him from poverty and bring him up in a comfortable Christian home. Then I do not believe that a child with what you call a 'criminal heredity' would be any more likely to become a criminal than any other child. It is poverty and bad conditions of environment that make criminals, not heredity.[2] Destroy poverty and you need not bother about criminal tendencies in chromosomes.[3]

P. If you destroy poverty, the problem will remain exactly

---

regarding himself as a philosopher are very slender. He obtained a third class in the Moral Sciences Tripos at Cambridge twenty years ago and has read little philosophy since then. This may, therefore, fairly be classed as an appeal to prestige based on false credentials (No 24).

[1] A question designed to draw out an admission damaging to C—'s case (No 27). The form of the question assumes that it would be necessary to imprison the child with criminal tendencies when he grows up, which would, of course, be denied by C—. The answer of either 'Yes' or 'No' to this question involves the acceptance of this assumption.

[2] Opposing P—'s extreme statement that criminal heredity always makes criminals with the equally extreme and equally untrue statement that it plays no part, but that poverty alone makes criminals. Again equivalent to the error of omitting 'some' and implying 'all' (No 2). Note too that C— has made a considerable shift of the ground of debate (No 6), now putting forward poverty (i.e. environmental conditions) instead of free-will in opposition to P—'s insistence on heredity. In fact the determination of conduct by environment has just the same difficulties for a theory of free-will as has its determination by heredity, so we must conclude that C— holds two sets of opinions on the subject which, while not necessarily inconsistent with one another, have not had their mutual implications thought out.

[3] Repeating three times in different words the statement about heredity and poverty (No 21).

the same.¹ Look at the rich criminals.² All the modern scientific work on heredity proves the importance of hereditary
factors in determining the behaviour of the individual.³

C.   All the best modern philosophy is agreed in stressing
the importance of the individual's free-will.⁴

P.   Philosophy is said to be the handmaid of theology, and
I have no doubt that philosophers are able to find excellent
reasons for a conception so useful to theology as free-will.⁵

¹ Again asserting the extreme and untrue opposite of C—'s proposition. The truth is that there is a positive association of crime with both
criminal heredity and poverty. P— and C— seem each equally incapable of thinking in terms of a tendency for B to follow from A (Chapter
II), so make either the extreme and untrue statement that all A is B or
that no A is B.

² An inconsequent argument (No 7) if it is intended as a proof of the
preceding statement, although it is a sound disproof of C—'s statement.
The fact that some criminals are not poor is not a proof that there is no
tendency for poverty to produce criminality, although it is a disproof of
the statement that poverty is the sole cause of crime.

³ Another diversion from an extreme to a moderate position. What
he now says is unquestionably true, but it is not what he said before.
Instead of leading inevitably to crime, heredity is now 'an important
factor'.

⁴ Another inconsequent argument (No 7). The statement that free-
will is important is not a denial of the importance of heredity, although
it is put forward as if it were. As is often the case, this inconsequent
argument also invites a diversion (No 6). In this argument authority
is opposed against authority, but with an important difference. P— is
appealing to the general conclusion to be drawn from all biological
experiment and observation. C—, on the other hand, is appealing to the
'best' philosophy. Even if P— were willing to admit that the philosophers had a method of establishing this conclusion of equal validity
with that of scientists, he would be suspicious of an appeal to the 'best'
philosophers. This means that the philosophers whose authority is to be
considered are to be selected. Their opinions on free-will will pretty
certainly be one of the marks by which it will be decided whether they
belong to the class of the 'best philosophers'. C—'s appeal to authority
is thus also a proof by selected instances (No 3).

⁵ Argument by the imputation of motives (No 38). P— is implying

For myself, I am more impressed by the fact that science rejects the conception.[1]

I should be interested to know how philosophers have managed to disprove a conclusion so soundly established experimentally as that of the importance of heredity.[2]

C. I can hardly hope to give an account of the present position of free-will in philosophy without taking some time over it. I am afraid this will not be of much interest to you, B—.

B. Well, you have been getting a little out of my depth lately. I wonder whether the truth doesn't lie between your ideas and P—'s, and perhaps heredity and a good home play an equal part in deciding whether a young lad will turn into a criminal.[3] But I should be most interested to hear what you have to say about free-will, very interested indeed.[4] Let me look at my watch.

---

that philosophers believe in free-will because they need the doctrine for theological purposes. C— might just as well retort by suggesting that scientists believe in heredity because they want to escape responsibility for their sins.

[1] Makes an appeal to science in the form of an appeal to mere authority (No 28), as C— did to the best philosophers. The word 'science' is here used vaguely and protects the argument in the same way as C—'s word 'best'. It is individual scientists and not science that gives opinions on free-will. Some of these have one opinion, some another. Some of the reasons they give for their opinions are good and some bad. The value of their opinions must be judged by the soundness of their reasons. It cannot be made a matter of appeal to their reasonable authority, since they have no better way of finding out the truth on this matter than the rest of us.

[2] Deals with C—'s inconsequent argument by asking for explanation as to how the conclusions of philosophers affect the question of heredity.

[3] True enough, although B— gives no better reason for it than the recommendation of a mean between two extremes (No 9). For the word 'equal' there can be no possible justification.

[4] B— reinforces this improbable statement by saying it three times (No 21).

Do you know, I really think we ought to be going up to the drawing-room. I hope you won't mind putting off the rest of this discussion to another evening. Most interesting. You won't mind, C—?

C.   Oh no, not at all. You have relieved me of a very difficult task. I have found it a very interesting evening, although I am afraid we have not settled any of the great problems we have been discussing.[1]

[1] With this statement at any rate we can find ourselves in complete agreement.

APPENDIX III

LIST OF BOOKS REFERRED TO
IN THE TEXT

p 10 Wittgenstein, L., *Philosophical Investigations*, Oxford, Basil Blackwell, 1958.

p 13 Lorenz, K., *On Aggression*, (Eng trans), London, Methuen, 1966.

p 16 Hall, Radclyffe, *The Well of Loneliness*, London, Falcon Press, 1928. (Reprinted, Corgi Books, 1968).

p 19 Charlton, H. B., *The Art of Literary Study*, London, Isaac Pitman & Sons, 1924.

p 50 Bentham, Jeremy, *The Theory of Fictions*, 1932.

p 53 Hobbes, T., *Leviathan*, London, A. Crooke, 1651, (Reprinted, Penguin Books, 1968).

p 53 Kropotkin, P. A., *Mutual Aid*, London, William Heinemann, 1902.

p 67 James, W., *Pragmatism*, London, Longmans, Green & Co, 1907.

p 84 De Bono, E., *Lateral Thinking: a text-book of creativity*, London, Spain Press, 1970.

p 88 Le Bon, G., *The Crowd: a study of the popular mind*, (Eng trans), London, T. Fisher Unwin, 1896.

p 109 Fielding, H., *The History of Tom Jones, a Foundling*, London, J. Bell, 1775.

p 113 Torrey, R. A., *How to promote and conduct a successful revival*, London, Andrew Melrose, 1901.

p 116 Goldsmith, O., *The Vicar of Wakefield*, London, F. Newbery, 1766.

p 119   Schopenhauer, A., *The Art of Controversy*, (Eng trans), London, Swan Sonnenschein & Co, 1896.

p 139   Nietzsche, F., *Thus Spake Zarathustra*, (Eng trans), London, George Allen & Unwin, 1967.

p 139   Russell, B., 'The Free Man's Worship', in *Philosophical Essays*, London, Longmans, Green & Co, 1910.

p 139   Marx, K., *Capital*, (Eng trans), London, Swan Sonnenschein, Lowrey & Co, 1887.

p 139   Mao, T., *The Political Thought of Mao Tse-tung*, (Eng trans), Harmondsworth, Penguin Books, 1969.

p 139   Greer, Germaine, *The Female Eunuch*, London, MacGibbon & Kee, 1970.

p 152   Hitler, A., *Mein Kampf*, (Eng trans), London, Hurst & Blackett, 1939.

p 152   *Protocols of the meetings of the learned Elders of Zion*, (Eng trans), London, Britons Publishing Society, 1931.

p 165   Montague, C. E., *Disenchantment*, London, Chatto & Windus, 1922.

p 176   *Mencius*, (Eng trans), Harmondsworth, Penguin Books, 1970.

p 181   Plato, *The Republic*, (Eng trans), London, J. M. Dent & Sons, 1906.

p 183   Wertheimer, M., *Productive Thinking*, (Eng trans), London, Tavistock Publications, 1961.

INDEX

John Nicholson
Habits £1.25

'Each chapter deals with something most of us do, consciously or unconsciously, every day — living with other people and our surroundings, eating, remembering, winning and losing, believing, walking, smoking, pretending . . . jargon is kept to a minimum . . . the book is elegant and restrained' SPECTATOR

'Marvellous and riveting . . . readable and funny . . . comes up with some fascinating answers'
VIRGINIA IRONSIDE, WOMAN'S WORLD

Peter Lauster
The Personality Test 70p

Stop being your own worst enemy — become the person you want to be. By completing Peter Lauster's ten tests you can learn to recognize your secret goals and desires ; discover the personality traits that hold you back from success and happiness. By affording you new and amazing insights into your own character this distinguished psychologist will help you to a fuller life.

Julius Fast
Body Language £1.50

Every move you make reveals a secret . . . This important book adds a new dimension to human understanding. Julius Fast teaches how to penetrate the personal secrets of strangers, friends and lovers by interpreting their body movements — and how to make use of the power thus gained.

Alvin Toffler
Future Shock £1.95

Future shock is the disease of change. Its symptoms are already here . . . *Future Shock* tells what happens to people overwhelmed by too rapid change . . . And looks at the human side of tomorrow.

Brilliantly disturbing, the book analyses the new and dangerous society now emerging, and shows how to come to terms with the future.

'An important book reaching some startling conclusions' BBC

'If this book is neglected we shall all be very foolish' C. P. SNOW

Thomas A. Harris MD
I'm OK – You're OK £1.50

A practical guide to Transactional Analysis. This phenomenal breakthrough in psychotherapy has proved a turning point for thousands of Americans.

An important new method of helping people, Transactional Analysis brings a refreshingly practical approach to the problems we all encounter in day-to-day relationships with ourselves and other people. In sensible, non-clinical language Thomas Harris tells how to gain control of your life and be responsible for your future – no matter what happened in the past.

Christopher Ward
How To Complain £1.25

A consumer's handbook with all the short cuts, plus addresses of those who can help you get results from : shops, garages, airlines, companies, landlords, banks, and most other sources of aggravation and exasperation.

'A lot of sound advice, laced with quite a few laughs'
KATIE BOYLE, TV TIMES

Reference, Language and Information

☐ Dictionary of Physical Sciences		£1.95p
☐ Everyman's Roget's Thesaurus		£1.95p
☐ The Limits to Growth		£1.50p
☐ Multilingual Commercial Dictionary		£1.95p
☐ Pan Dictionary of Synonyms and Antonyms		£1.95p
☐ Pan English Dictionary		£2.50p
☐ Universal Encyclopaedia of Mathematics		£2.95p

Literature Guides

☐ An Introduction to Shakespeare and his Contemporaries	Marguerite Alexander	£1.50p
☐ An Introduction to Fifty American Poets	Peter Jones	£1.75p
☐ An Introduction to Fifty American Novels	Ian Ousby	£1.95p
☐ An Introduction to Fifty British Novels 1600–1900	Gilbert Phelps	£2.50p
☐ An Introduction to Fifty British Poets 1300–1900	Michael Schmidt	£1.95p
☐ An Introduction to Fifty Modern British Poets		£1.50p
☐ An Introduction to Fifty European Novels	Martin Seymour-Smith	£1.95p
☐ An Introduction to Fifty British Plays 1660–1900	John Cargill Thompson	£1.95p